The Simple *Joy* of Seeing God

A.J. SPURR

Ark House Press
PO Box 1722, Port Orchard, WA 98366 USA
PO Box 1321, Mona Vale NSW 1660 Australia
PO Box 318 334, West Harbour, Auckland 0661 New Zealand
arkhousepress.com

© A.J. SPURR 2021

Unless otherwise stated, all Scriptures are taken from the Message version of the bible. Some names and identifying details have been changed to protect the privacy of individuals.

Cataloguing in Publication Data:
Title: The Simple Joy Of Seeing God
ISBN: 978-0-6452277-1-0 (pbk)
Subjects: Christian Living;
Other Authors/Contributors: Spurr, A.J.

Design by initiateagency.com

Acknowledgements

Thank you to my husband Phil, who walks this journey beside me.

My Tyson and my Jack - I'm eternally grateful for you both. You have taught me so much more about life and love than I could ever hope to teach you.

My dad, John for editing and advising me on this literary adventure, and my mother, Joan - my love for words was birthed on your lap, as your read to me every night.

Contents

A Chronic Lack of Awe	1
The Secret Password	9
The Avatar Effect	16
In Everything?	27
Lipstick on Your Teeth	38
Showing Up	48
Grateful Giving	63
Divine Forgiveness	71
The Antidote to Fear	76
Practice Makes Perfect	87
The God Who Sees Me	94
Supernatural Satisfaction	104
Bibliography	117

Introduction

As a freelance writer, I've been blessed with incredible opportunities to write blogs and articles about a number of fascinating topics. One of my favourite projects has been researching and writing articles for Australia's National Day of Thanks, across more than a decade. What I learnt about the power and spiritual significance of gratitude during that time has changed my life.

I've also interviewed countless ex-prisoners and people who have overcome drug and alcohol addiction, whose lives were transformed when they experienced personal encounters with Jesus. Time after time, they speak about how so many of us on the 'outside' are living in prisons we've created for ourselves. Prisons of unforgiveness, fear, anger and hate.

A few years ago, I felt God put on my heart the passion to write about what my research has uncovered, which has left such an indelible mark on my life. But like so many, I lived with crippling self-doubt.

I cried out to God and said, "if you really want me to write this book, please show me."

A few days later I was at church on a Sunday morning and our pastor invited each of us to come forward for a word of encouragement. A group of church leaders lined the foot of the stage and I had my eye on a mature, older woman who I wanted to speak over me but there was quite a line of women waiting to speak to her. My husband nudged me and pointed to a young woman who I'd never seen before (and have never seen since!). "You need to speak to *her*," he said.

Reluctantly, I stepped forward and stood silently in front of this stranger. She put her hand on my arm and we were silent together, for what seemed like an eternity. 'Well, this is awkward,' I thought. 'She doesn't have a word for me.'

I was just about to save both of us from my embarrassment by thanking her for her silent prayer and walking back to my seat, when she finally spoke. "You see beautiful things and you really notice them," she said. "This is a reflection of God's thumbprint on your heart. You will show people how to see these beautiful things in a unique way that no one's ever done before."

Tears filled my eyes.

"Does that mean anything to you?" She asked.

"Oh yes!" I responded. God had just shown me so clearly what He wanted me to do.

This is a book about seeing God, who is beautiful, learning to see His invisible qualities (Romans 1:20) and being aware of His presence in every circumstance.

It's also a book about a *seeing* God. A God who sees you in every circumstance. And how that changes everything.

A Chronic Lack of Awe

A FEW YEARS AGO, ONE of the biggest rock bands in the world committed an unprecedented act of generosity.

One September morning, 500 million music lovers around the world awoke to discover U2's album, 'Songs of Innocence' automatically downloaded to their Apple iTunes music library. This was in the days prior to online music streaming, when CDs were on the way out and people were embracing this new way of consuming their favourite tunes. Songs and albums had to be purchased and then downloaded to your Apple iPod before you could listen to them.

So, receiving an entire album for *free* was a pretty big deal.

What was the response to this unexpected gift from one of the world's biggest bands…?

Complete, utter, unmitigated fury! Millions took to social media, expressing their rage and even disgust at being subjected to U2's music against their will.

The collective international furore forced iTunes to create a specific 'U2 Removal Tool,' allowing users to 'hand back' the unwanted gift with one click.

This moment quietly defined a generation and has become synonymous with the 'Age of Entitlement,' in which whatever we desire is a 'right,' rather than a privilege. Where we don't have to pretend to be thankful for what we have, because we earnt it, right? And we're cheered on for demanding what we want.

With most Western families now earning two incomes, saying 'no' to children's demands has become a matter of choice, rather than necessity.

Many parents 'cave in,' rather than risk subjecting themselves to another tantrum, for the sake of sanity and serenity. But at what cost?

Growing up, my father was a pastor earning below minimum wage. We lived without most of the excesses many of my friends enjoyed at home. No microwave, or dishwasher, no brand label clothes and definitely no expensive toys for myself or my three brothers. My parents rarely needed to say 'no' to anything because we knew better than to ask.

But there was this one time when we all banded together with a common desire… a VCR (video player)!

We started a 'savings jar.' Every week, we deposited our pocket money into the jar, and mum and dad added to it as they could. Until one day, mum counted up our dollars and cents and yes, we'd done it! We finally had enough money to purchase the long awaited, much anticipated VCR!

I'll never forget the afternoon we came home from school and kneeled in a circle around the unopened box. Dad offered up a prayer of thanks for this incredible blessing and we sat in a moment of silent awe.

Then, we walked excitedly to the video store around the corner together, and hired out the newly released 'The Gods Must Be Crazy.' It was glorious.

Whenever we went away on holidays, the VCR was unplugged and hidden under a bed for safe keeping. It was so precious to us, and we were so grateful for it, because we knew how much it cost.

Today, most western kids have an iPad each, a TV in just about every room and movies 'on-demand.' They don't even have to sit through ad breaks, or wait until next week for the next episode of their favourite show. They'll never know the agony and ecstasy of real anticipation.

One of the basics of parenting is teaching our children to say 'please' and 'thank you,' but rather than perfunctory manners, how do we teach them to *experience* the joy of gratitude?

If you've ever been to the birthday party of a small child, you'll know the embarrassment of watching them open a gift they didn't want. Especially if their parent has forgotten to remind them of the official birthday mantra: "You get what you get and you don't get upset."

I remember buying a birthday gift for a friend's little girl and when I received the mandatory 'thank you' phone call, I noticed a distinct *edge* in her little voice.

"Did you like your gift?" I asked. She had wanted a 'Shopkins' set and I had selected one I thought she would really like.

"You bought the wrong one," she responded, her anger tangible over the phone line.

"Oh," I said, flabbergasted. "Well, it's the thought that counts."

"Think *better* next time," she retorted, and ended the call.

Still holding the phone to my ear, I chuckled to myself. I could picture God listening to me whinging whenever I felt he'd given me a dud gift. Then later realising that what He'd given me was just what I needed.

But what about when a child tears open the wrapping paper to reveal that thing they *really* want, hand delivered by a relative? Their face lights up with the glow of a dream fulfilled. Then we watch them run off in excitement to show their friends, with nary a backward glance. Are they *really* grateful if they love the gift, but don't acknowledge the gift giver? I'll talk about this more in chapter 2.

Perhaps gratitude can only be truly learnt by experiencing lack. Perhaps it's only then that we can truly appreciate the value of what we have.

In our second year of marriage, my husband wanted to take me camping. I'm more of a '3-4 star hotel' kinda girl, but I acquiesced. As we set up our campsite, I fought the urge to throw everything into the boot and hightail it back to civilisation. Walking 20 metres to the toilet block felt so undignified and even inhumane. There's really no excuse for camp showers – nowhere to put your clean clothes to keep them dry and then there's the feeling of mouldy tiles underfoot, oozing with the promise of tinea.

Cue the rain.

It rained for days and so we cocooned ourselves inside our meagre tent, playing Solitaire and generally feeling damp. As soon as the rain receded to a drizzle, we hired a small boat with an outboard motor to traverse the meandering river.

We had a lovely afternoon exploring the estuaries, but the 'drop toilets' along the banks made our camp toilets seem positively palatial. It was right on sunset when our outboard motor fell eerily silent and we realised we were stranded in the middle of shark infested waters, a fresh burst of rain slowly filling our boat.

"We are going to die." I said, with conviction. "We are going to die and our tragic story will feature on the Late News."

Hopeless, exhausted, freezing, soaked through to my aching bones, and scooping water from our tiny boat with my hands, suddenly I looked up to see our salvation making its way towards us, in the shape of a tour boat.

Euphoria and relief overflowed down my cheeks as tears momentarily warmed my shivering soul. Towed to shore, we walked gingerly to our tent - now a veritable palace of dry and warmth. I picked up my fresh, dry clothes and buried my face in them, breathing in their promise of comfort as I squelched my way to the shower block. I turned on the hot tap and stepped under the shower head in a state of sheer elation. Warmth and comfort showered over my body. There was nothing else in that moment. I've never felt such gratitude in all my life.

A truly grateful heart is one that inhabits a perpetual state of awe and wonder.

Your eye is a lamp, lighting up your whole body. If you live wide-eyed in wonder and belief, your body fills up with light. If you live squinty-eyed in greed and distrust, your body is a dank cellar.' Luke 11:34

See the blessing even in the mundane; like the light that fills a dark room at the flick of a switch, the singing of a kettle whose contents are ready to bring you warmth, and the chorus of birds announcing the possibilities of a new day.

Every moment offers a new gift; it's up to you to receive it, with thanks.

Like the Tax Collector who stood before God. Who, overcome by humility and gratitude, could barely believe that the Creator of the universe would deign to gift him life (Luke 18:9-14).

Have you ever wondered why days seemed to last forever when you were a child... and now it feels like you blink and another week's over?

The pace of life is faster than ever. Technology has made life easier, if not simpler, yet there's no invention that can slow down time.

The truth is, we're suffering from a chronic lack of awe. The one thing that makes time stop, for a moment, is when you pause to notice and reflect.

In one [1]study, people who watched scenes that inspired awe (waterfalls, whales, space walks etc) agreed with statements like "I have lots of time in which I can get things done" and "Time is expanded."

The journey from entitlement to gratitude begins with a simple, conscious choice to inhabit each moment, to recognise each gift as it's offered, to acknowledge the Gift Giver, and to experience true joy in receiving it.

We're not the first generation to suffer from a chronic lack of awe. It dates back to the beginning of humanity.

I recently read the book of Exodus again, and it astounded me afresh how much the Israelites suffered from this condition…

They watched on as water turned to blood, frogs invaded the Egyptian's homes, there were lice, flies, and pestilence as far as the eye could see, followed by boils, hail, locusts and days of darkness for the Egyptians, while their camp was bathed in light. Surely the killing of the first born (except those with lamb's blood on their door frame) was the pinnacle of God's miraculous power and a sign of His protection over His people?

He led them out of slavery in a cloud by day and fire by night (*aw*esome, right?). But even after God gave a step-by-step guide as to what was about to take place; e.g. Pharaoh changing his mind, coming after them and His army meeting their untimely demise (Exodus 14:1-4), the Israelites instantly forgot everything they'd seen and heard.

In what might be the first documented example of biblical sarcasm, they said to Moses "Weren't the cemeteries large enough in Egypt so that you had to take us out here in the wilderness to die?" Exodus 14:10-12.

Despite their sass, God parted the waters of the sea (Exodus 14:15-16) with such care that they walked across to safety on dry sand. It's a small detail I often miss but the Israelites didn't have to walk through any puddles, or even a patch of mud. God made the ground beneath their feet, just moments before covered by unrelenting ocean, completely dry, flanked by a giant aquarium on either side. Wouldn't you have just loved to be there to experience that?

Yes, they celebrated and were filled with awe but after following cloud and fire like it was totally no big deal for three more days, they were back to complaining again. They said, *"So what are we supposed to drink?"* Exodus 15:24

And so it went for forty years. God would do something incredible like raining down bread and quails from heaven (Exodus 16:11-12), and they would show they still didn't quite trust Him (vs 19-20). They would be thankful for a little while, then go back to their default position of grumbling.

Every time Moses turned his back, the Israelites were complaining, or worshipping idols. And when they finally arrived at the entrance to the Promised Land, after 40 years of miracles and provision from God, they had long forgotten the plagues, the parting of the sea, the manna, the drinking water, the stone tablets from heaven, the cloud and fire guiding their path. Their sense of awe and wonder was quenched, and they were stalled by fear. Except for two men, Joshua and Caleb, who remembered God's faithfulness and His miracles, and trusted Him to defeat a seemingly insurmountable enemy.

In Numbers 13:16 there's a spoiler alert. Joshua wasn't always called Joshua. His original name was Hoshea, meaning 'Salvation.' But before sending him to scout the Promised Land, Moses changes his name to Joshua, meaning 'God Saves.' Giving honour to the One who brings Salvation is the secret to truly receiving it.

The Secret Password

———

IT COULD BE A COMBINATION of your dog's name, your anniversary and your first child's birth date. Get it right and you're in. Get it wrong – and you can be locked out. Forever.

Your password is the key that opens the virtual doorway to your bank accounts, emails, Social Media profiles and holiday bookings. If you've ever forgotten your password, you know the frustration of security questions (what was the name of my first dog again?) and waiting impatiently for the Password Reset email, enabling you to create a new password consisting of upper and lower case letters… and at least 2 numbers. How are you supposed to remember *that*?

When security consultant Mark Burnett compiled a list of the top 10,000 most common passwords, he discovered that the number one password people used was 'password.' The second was '123456.'

Did you know that there's a password that takes you into the presence of God? And it's no secret, yet many people never use it. It's not hexadecimal, alphanumeric or encrypted, yet it's quickly forgotten.

No one ever told me the password, God revealed it to me.

In the Old Testament, only one person, the High Priest, was allowed to experience God's presence and only once a year. It was a reminder that no one was allowed to just 'walk in on God.'

'Under this system, the gifts and sacrifices can't really get to the heart of the matter, can't assuage the conscience of the people, but are limited to matters of ritual and behaviour. It's essentially a temporary arrangement until a complete overhaul could be made.'
Hebrews 9:7-9

The inner chamber of the sanctuary in the Jewish Temple in Jerusalem was separated by a veil from the outer chamber. It was reserved for the presence of God and could be entered only by the High Priest on the Day of Atonement.

But then… Jesus. The 'Great High Priest.'

At some point in your life, you've probably prayed the Lord's Prayer: "Our Father, who art in Heaven…" and so on.

But in the original Aramaic, it can be translated as: "To my Father who is as close to me as the air I breathe, I stop and become aware of you."

That. Changes. Everything. A distant, far away God is suddenly closer than your closest friend.

Every now and then, something divine happens that takes you completely by surprise and leaves you revelling in the ethereal afterglow.

One night at a church prayer meeting, I was overwhelmed by a deep sense of gratitude toward God. I revelled in His goodness and reflected on the blessings in my life.

As I stood in awe, eyes closed, whispering 'thank you, thank you, thank you God,' over and over again, suddenly I saw Jesus. He was sitting on a chair in front of me, glorious rainbow colours emanating from His body and a thin, sheer veil was all that lay between us.

"Dare I ask it?" I whispered. "Could I ... really ... come into your presence, Jesus?"

With that, the veil lifted, and I was standing before Him, unobstructed.

Overcome, I asked myself; 'What's the appropriate response when you're in the presence of Jesus? Should I bow, or fall to my knees, or lay prostrate before Him?'

Worried that I was doing it all wrong, I looked into His face and heard His voice gently say, 'I can see your gratitude. That's the appropriate response.'

It wasn't until weeks later that I read Psalm 100:4-5 and had a fresh revelation: *'Enter with the password: "Thank you!" Make yourselves at home, talking praise. Thank Him. Worship Him. For God is sheer beauty, all-generous in love, loyal always and ever.'*

It dawned on me that I wasn't just thankful to be in His presence, I was in His presence *because* I was thankful.

Although expressing gratitude towards God doesn't usually transport you into the throne room in a physical sense, in a spiritual sense it draws you closer to Him. Philippians 4:6 says *...'in every situation, by prayer and petition, with* *thanksgiving, present your requests to God.'* (NIV). Often, we focus on the 'prayer and petition' part and forget to say a heartfelt 'thanks' for what He has done and what He's about to do.

'Do you see what we've got? An unshakable kingdom! And do you see how thankful we must be? Not only thankful, but brimming with worship, deeply reverent before God.' Hebrews 12:29

I once shared a quote on social media: 'Imagine if you woke up today with only the things you thanked God for yesterday.' These words were a beautiful reminder to me that I should never take any heavenly gift for granted.

Someone commented, 'I will not be guilted into feeling thankful!' That really sums up the sentiment of our 'entitled' generation and the attitude that's robbing us (myself included at times) from experiencing an intimate relationship with God.

After all, if you're not overcome by a deep sense of gratitude for all He has done for you, you need to wake up to His goodness and get a fresh revelation; *'Open your mouth and taste, open your eyes and see— how good God is. Blessed are you who run to him.'* Psalm 34:8

Read Luke 17:11-19, the story of the ten lepers. Ten were healed by Jesus, only one was saved.

The one leper who said thank you was 'made well' (The Greek word in the original text is sozo: 'To be healed of spiritual disease and death'), the others were merely 'healed' (tharizo: 'To be made clean or healed of a physical disease'). Physical healing and spiritual healing (Salvation) are not the same thing. The difference is gratitude.

So, we haven't truly received God's gift of 'sozo' salvation until we are thankful for it.

This is the great secret of salvation. When we consider grace (the undeserved gift), our gratitude toward the Gift Giver (God) brings Him glory, and us joy. In chapter 1, I mentioned watching a child opening a gift they really wanted, then running away without acknowledging the Gift Giver. True gratitude is receiving the gift and acknowledging the Gift Giver, with heartfelt thanks.

'All this is for your benefit, so that the grace that is reaching more and more people may cause thanksgiving to overflow to the glory of God.' 2 Corinthians 4:15 (NIV)

It can't be a 'ritual and behaviour' – it has to 'get to the heart of the matter.' And what's the heart of the matter? The fact that God drew near to us in the form of a baby, who came to die the most excruciating and humiliating death imaginable, so that we might have life to the full and relationship with Him. The only appropriate response to this revelation is gratitude. A perfunctory, emotionless prayer doesn't cut it. Only a heartfelt expression of gratitude will draw you into His presence.

'Embracing what God does for you is the best thing you can do for him.' Romans 12:1-2

'But if anyone loves God [with awe-filled reverence, obedience and gratitude], he is known by Him [as His very own and is greatly loved].' 1 Corinthians 8:3 (AMP)

Psalm 22:3 also talks about God inhabiting the praises of His people.

And this is personified in a very real sense in 2 Chronicles by Jehoshaphat. When Moabites, Ammonites and Meunites joined forces to wage war against Jehoshaphat, he prayed and ordered a nationwide fast. Then he arranged a Praise Party.

2 Chronicles 20:21-24 says, *"After talking it over with the people, Jehoshaphat appointed a choir for God; dressed in holy robes, they were to march ahead of the troops, singing, Give thanks to God, His love never quits. As soon as they started shouting and praising, God set ambushes against the men of Ammon, Moab, and Mount Seir as they were attacking Judah, and they all ended up dead. The Ammonites and Moabites mistakenly attacked those from Mount Seir and massacred them. Then, further confused, they went at each other, and all ended up killed. As Judah came up over the rise, looking into the wilderness for the horde of barbarians, they looked on a killing field of dead bodies—not a living soul among them.'*

Something about their 'shouting and praising' activated God's plan for their salvation.

Let's talk about Jonah for a minute. After spending three days inside a fish, he finally started praising God. In Jonah 2:9, he says, *"I'm worshiping you, God, calling out in thanksgiving! And I'll do what I promised I'd do! Salvation belongs to God!"* Literally the next thing that happens is that God speaks to the fish and it releases Jonah, not into the depths of the ocean, but on the shore! Three days' walk from the city of Ninevah.

And right before David takes on Goliath, he bravely declares *"God, who delivered me from the teeth of the lion and the claws of the bear, will deliver me from this Philistine."* 1 Samuel 17:37

If you're feeling distant from your Creator, if you're facing insurmountable Giants, ask yourself: 'When did I last bask in His goodness and let His mercies pour over me? When did I last make myself at home talking praise, thanking Him, worshiping Him? When's the last time I arranged a Praise Party?'

The Avatar Effect

'AND DON'T BE WISHING YOU were someplace else or with someone else. Where you are right now is God's place for you. Live and obey and love and believe right there. God, not your marital status, defines your life.' 1 Corinthians 7:17

It was a blockbuster movie, taking over $1billion at the box office.

Avatar took viewers on an epic journey to Pandora - a fantasy world inhabited by a tribe of blue aliens called the Na'vi. Thanks to stunning visual effects, extraordinary plants and animals were brought to life amongst a breathtaking imaginary landscape.

With the help of 3D glasses, the line between fantasy and reality is blurred, making it feel as though you're actually sitting beneath the 'Tree of Souls' with the Na'vi tribe. But James Cameron's 'Avatar' had an unexpected effect on movie-goers.

After watching the movie, rather than relishing its cinematic escapism, many entered a state of depression.

Soon after its release, thousands of fans took to online forums, discussing 'The Avatar Effect.' One user wrote: *'When I woke up this morning after watching Avatar for the first time yesterday, the world seemed grey. It just seems so meaningless.'*

'Post Avatar Depression, also known as P.A.D. for short, is the case when a person after seeing the movie "Avatar" (By James Cameron) eventually realises that the world they live in sucks a** and that they will never be able to fly, jump or live like the Na'vi do on Pandora.' - The Urban Dictionary.

P.A.D. sufferers were caught in their own fantasy world of 'what ifs,' rather than appreciating 'what is.'

They saw only the beauty of Pandora, forgetting that if they were granted one night in its lush rainforest, they would likely encounter Pandora's terrifying wildlife, including viperwolves or Thanator-the super-predator with superpowers, not to mention the glowing plants that shoot poison leaf tips.

And soon they'd notice that most of Pandora's flora and fauna emit only one single colour; often green, blue, indigo, or violet, which is sure to get pretty 'ho hum' after a while. Would that change their outlook?

Here on 'boring old' Earth, there are 270,000 species of flowers, of too many colours to name, or even guess, as well as around 10,000 species of birds and around 60,000 species of trees. You could spend your entire life exploring the wonders of creation on Earth and still die before encountering them all.

Here are just a few for you to research and marvel at: Nacreous clouds, starling murmurations, bioluminescent waves, calcifying lakes, Russian light pillars, fire rainbows, brinicles, The Eye of the Sahara, frozen methane bubbles in Canada, Pink Lake in Australia, and my absolute favourite at the very top of my 'Bucket List' – Aurora Borealis and Aurora Australis.

Then look into the Fibonacci Sequence in nature and you'll discover a mathematical and creative genius who left His indelible handprint on creation.

Fibonacci Sequence can be seen in the structure of galaxies and flowers, fingerprints, snail shells and even the ovary of an Anglerfish. Much like the signature of a great artist in the corner of a canvas.

'Attention, all! See the marvels of God! He plants flowers and trees all over the earth... "Step out of the traffic! Take a long, loving look at me, your High God, above politics, above everything."' Psalm 46:8-10

A few years ago, I did what many young people do; I embarked on my own journey of discovery, backpacking through Europe.

Sitting in my economy class seat on the plane, I felt like a kid in a candy store! There were more movie options than I had flight time to watch. As you might have guessed by my reverence for our family VCR, I'm a bit of a movie buff. I love the art of storytelling and giving life to imagination.

Perhaps it's because I grew up in a world where gorillas can talk and deliver food! Let me explain…

My parents were missionaries in the mountains of Lebanon during the civil war. My mother recalls one day hanging out washing, with my older brother (an infant at the time) sitting in the grass at her feet. Suddenly, she heard gunfire as two men started shooting over her head toward an enemy below. Instantly she fell to the ground, sheltering her baby, but then adrenaline and 'mother bear instincts' kicked in. She stood to her feet, fists clenched and shouted, "What are you trying to do? Kill each other as well as a mother and a child? Shame on you both!" They paused, stunned by her boldness, then shrugged their shoulders and walked away.

Soon after, the fighting intensified and my parents had to leave everything and flee to the airport, hoping to fly out of the war zone. But there were no flights departing due to the fighting and they found themselves stranded in the airport lounge. Years later, my mother told me about the kindly guerrillas who brought them food and made sure they were safe. Of course, it didn't occur to mum to explain to my 4-year-old self that guerrillas are human soldiers. So, wide eyed and filled with awe, I vividly pictured giant gorillas talking to my parents and bringing them sustenance, probably in the form of bananas.

I proudly shared with my classmates my knowledge about talking gorillas at show-and-tell one day, and my teacher sat bemused, shaking her head, as I adamantly defended the veracity of my story. My parents told me that's what happened, and they never lie, so how dare my teacher say it can't be true! I think I was nearly 10 before the penny dropped. It was around the time I discovered that clouds were not in fact giant fluffy marshmallows, inviting me to bounce amongst their fairy-floss softness. I was devastated. But a little girl who lives in a world inhabited by talking gorillas and bouncy clouds can't help but develop an awe-filled outlook.

Thanks to my older brother, I also lived in a world of 'drop bears' and 'hoop snakes' but that's another story.

Shortly after arriving in London, I hopped on a tour bus headed for Edinburgh, via the idyllic Lakes District. The first stop on the tour was an ancient castle. It was spectacular! I shook my head at my fellow travellers who had opted to stay on the bus and miss experiencing it.

It reminded me of a time when I was about 5 years old, living in the Arabian Gulf. My mother had befriended one of Yasser Arafat's nieces and she invited us to her palatial home for coffee.

I sat cross-legged on a mat, with an opulent buffet of exotic treats laid out on magnificent rugs in front of us. I was on my very best behaviour and mum even let me try a sip of her Turkish Coffee. I still remember its rich aroma and strong, dark taste in my mouth. To me, this was a life changing experience, but to everyone else in the room, it was just another meal and just another cup of coffee.

Back to the tour, somewhere between London and Edinburgh… I spent the entire hour allotted for the castle visit in awe, touching every stone in reach and taking countless photographs. I gazed up at the turrets, marvelling at the ancient technology that held them in place. It was like standing on a page of a history book, and I imagined the stories that had been written here hundreds of years ago.

The second stop was another castle. I took a few photos and enjoyed the picturesque view.

The third stop was another castle. I walked around for a few minutes and got back on the bus.

The fourth stop was another castle. It was cold. I stayed on the bus.

What had changed? As our tour guide said when most of us opted to stay on the bus at the next stop: "Seen one castle, seen 'em all."

On another tour bus, we stopped in Bath and I was in awe as I meandered through the ancient Roman baths. Walking along the cobbled streets, completely enamoured with this historic place, I spotted a boy in his dishevelled school uniform walking listlessly beside his harried mother. I wanted to scream out 'How can you just *exist* in this incredible place?!' How could they just carry on as if they lived in a boring place like where I'd travelled from? Just doing life; going to school, work, and play dates. How could that mother feel 'harried' in a place of historical significance like this? Why was this boy staring at his shoes when there were ancient artefacts just 'lying around?' Could it be that they, too, were once in awe of this place and just stopped seeing it? In the busyness of life, it became just another place. And perhaps now they dreamed of lands far away from here, where they would no longer feel harried and insignificant, just as I had back home.

Have you ever watched a newborn discover their hand for the first time? It's mesmerising. They slowly turn their wrist, then watch in wonder as each finger, one by one, moves by the power of their mind, their eyes as wide as dinner plates at the sheer wonder of it. Then they discover their feet and toes and the slow, awe filled dance continues.

But then one day, their hands and feet are just 'there.' No longer mesmerising, just existing without fanfare.

Recently, a friend severed the top of his finger and it had to be surgically reattached. His whole finger was wrapped up tight for weeks while it healed. When it was finally unwrapped, his fingertip was so sensitive to touch, like electricity running through his hand, he had to get used to it all over again. I imagine that's what it feels like for newborns; every touch like electricity, until their brain and senses adapt.

The fact is, if we spent our days staring at the wonder of our hands, and feeling electricity at every touch, we wouldn't get very much done, so our brains have a 'block out' system, ensuring we only notice what's 'necessary' at the time. It's why you can drive home from work and have no recollection of the journey. Your brain is on 'auto-pilot' in familiar surroundings. But it's on high alert, taking in every street name and landmark when you're driving in unfamiliar territory. If we took in every piece of information thrown at us each day, our brains would not cope.

It means that noticing things which have become familiar doesn't come easily. We have to consciously make an effort to notice and strive not to lose the wonder in the familiar. Being transformed, as it were, by the daily renewing our minds (Romans 12:2).

I asked some friends what they would love to experience for the first time again, just to feel that sense of awe and wonder they'd lost in the familiarity of it. Here are some of their responses:

Watching The Lord of The Rings trilogy.
Visiting The Grand Canyon.
The moment I held my babies for the first time.
Going to Disney Land.

My first solo around the world trip! I did it with the eyes and mind of a mid-20's something girl and now almost 20 years later I'd love to see it all again.

Seeing things with fresh eyes and genuinely appreciating what you have is the secret to reversing the 'Avatar Effect.' After all, if you don't feel grateful for what you already have, what makes you think you'll be happy with something else?

'You're blessed when you get your inside world – your mind and heart – put right. Then you can see God in the outside world.' Matthew 5:8

A few years ago, I started experiencing back and neck pain. I'd wake up every morning feeling like I'd been run over by a truck. I tried four or five different pillows and we even replaced the mattress, but nothing seemed to make any difference.

Finally, I took a friend's advice and visited a Chiropractor. An X-Ray revealed that my neck, which should be curved, was almost dead straight, my hips were twisted, and I had a mild case of scoliosis. It wouldn't have mattered **what** I changed in the environment around me, the issue was *inside.*

The adjustments felt like a roller coaster ride and I let out a 'whoop' with every 'crack.' Every instinct in my body rebelled against each spine cracking movement and the Chiropractor waited patiently while I calmed myself sufficiently to facilitate the next seemingly unnatural motion.

I walked into the Chiropractor's office hunched over and in pain, I walked out feeling on top of the world! "I can't believe this is how I was meant to be feeling all along," I told the receptionist, beaming. "And I'd just lived with this pain thinking it was normal."

How often we think 'If only I had her job...' or 'his house...' or 'their kids...' then I'd be happy. The fact is that our happiness should never be determined by our 'happenings,' but instead by finding wholeness within and taking time to see the beauty around us.

As the old saying goes: 'It's not happy people who are grateful, it's grateful people who are happy.' If there's something we can learn from sufferers of Post Avatar Depression, it's that we shouldn't let what we want, alter our view of what we have.

Giving birth is no time for humour, but that didn't stop my obstetrician when I was in labour with my second child. As I gasped and groaned, he leaned over to the nurse and said: 'this is the one who doesn't like exercise.' Then he grinned at me and said 'I bet you're regretting it now...'

I was too exhausted to yell at him but also, I knew he was right. When does a busy working mum fit in exercise?

It was a couple of years later, having gained nearly 20 kilograms during my child-bearing season, that I decided it was time to get back into shape. Running around after two toddlers was tiring, especially if you're unfit.

So, one afternoon I dusted off my sneakers, checked them for cobwebs and decided to go for a jog.

"I'll be back in half an hour," I called out. And right on cue, two pairs of feet came scrambling down the hallway.

"Can we come too?" Tyson squealed, excitedly. Jack looked up at me with those hard-to-say-no-to eyes. My shoulders slumped.

"Mummy just needs some time out... to exercise."

"Please, mummy?" He begged. Those eyes. Sigh.

I got out the two-seater pram and they both clambered in. I started to think it might actually be a good idea – giving my arms a good work-out, as well as my legs. That is, until we got about 2 metres down the road and Tyson yelled urgently: "Stop mummy!" He said it with so much passion I was sure I'd run over something dreadful. Hastily, he jumped out of the pram and declared "look mum, a stick!"

Proud as punch, he jumped back into the pram, brandishing his new stick in the direction of his brother, and I took a few more steps. I hadn't even hit my stride yet when Jack yelled out: "Slow down! I need a stick too, mummy!"

I slowed to just above crawling speed as we scoured the footpath for a decent sized stick.

Once found, we were off again. We actually travelled a good 25 metres before Tyson yelled out again "STOP!"

Okay, I was starting to lose my patience. How's a girl supposed to get her heart rate up with all this stopping? "What is it *now*?" I muttered impatiently.

I turned to see what all the fuss was about, to find Tyson smiling sweetly. "For you, mummy," he grinned, holding up a little bunch of wildflowers. How had I not noticed them before? I suppose I'd never really stopped to look.

And so it was that my 'heart pumping' workout morphed into a treasure hunt. My boys took me on a guided tour of 'hidden treasures' around our neighbourhood. They knew where all the wildflowers were. Gradually, I went from 'harried' to happy and completely 'in the moment.' I thought back to that mum in Bath. Perhaps I had been a bit 'judgey.' After all, I'd just been 'existing' in a beautiful place, too.

I may never smell the flowers on Pandora but I've learnt that the flowers here on Earth are pretty special too, once I took the time to smell them.

In Everything?

Give thanks in *everything* (1 Thessalonians 8:13)?

Everything? Even the **bad** things? That seems a bit much. Completely unrealistic and unfair. That's what I thought, anyway... Until a near tragedy changed my point of view.

It started out like most nights at our place... frantically getting dinner ready while my boys played noisily around my feet. Phil had just stepped outside to light the barbeque when we heard an almighty 'thud!'

I absently thought to myself 'what on earth was that?' Then Phil and I looked at each other and the horror in his eyes made my heart sink with realisation... Jack (just 2 days shy of his first birthday) had found a small gap in the staircase hand rail and plunged, head first, 2 ½ metres to the wooden floor below.

I froze. "He's dead." I mouthed the words because I couldn't speak them. "There's no way he survived that," I whispered. A myriad of unspeakable thoughts went through my mind. It seemed like a million years passed, but it was only a moment. Then, miraculously, a cry rose up from below. 'He's alive!' Phil defied gravity as he flew down the stairs and instinctively picked up our baby boy.

I was already on the phone, calling an ambulance. Jack's forehead had doubled in size and was distinctly purple. The operator finally made sense of my hysteria and an ambulance was on its way.

Running out the door, Jack screaming in my arms, our neighbours casually leaned over the fence for a chat and realised all was not well. Phil was holding Jack's older brother, Tyson (poor, confused Tyson) and he explained the situation.

Jenni ran inside, shouting over her shoulder "I'm coming in the ambulance with you!" How grateful I was to have someone with me who could talk sensibly to the medics while Phil and Tyson followed behind in our car.

At the hospital, a good half a dozen emergency medical staff were waiting for us to arrive and they pounced on Jack.

X-rays, MRIs, a cannula, poking and prodding. I sang to him in a desperate, broken voice, trying to keep him calm. I was falling apart but the nurses were so gentle and kind with me.

Meanwhile, Phil had texted everyone we knew, asking them to pray for our little Jack.

By midnight, he was fast asleep. I was set up on a trundle bed beside him and I sat there, at 2am, staring out at the beautiful city lights as texts and emails poured in from friends and family who were praying for Jack.

Phil's sister was already on her way to help him with Tyson at home and my mother came and sat with me in the Neurology Ward for two days, so that I could have a shower, or just go for a walk and clear my head.

Day 2 was Jack's first birthday. His party had been, understandably, cancelled but he was smiling; a bruised, black-eyed smile, and nothing else mattered in the whole wide world.

Finally, at about 3pm that day, a Neurologist gave him the all clear. "Just a large fracture from the top of his head to his eye socket." Ouch!

The sense of relief was incredible. Mum drove us home and as I took my first step inside, I burst into tears. I didn't know anything about Post-Traumatic Stress Syndrome but that's what I was experiencing. For weeks, whenever I heard an ambulance siren or a loud 'thud' I would jump ten feet in the air. Tyson became super protective of his little brother – running from the other side of the house to make sure Jack was okay whenever he cried.

My social media post, written the day we arrived home from the hospital says it all: *"When something terrible happens, that's when you realize love is tangible. It has a face and hands, it's a kind voice, it's prayers, it's words, it's presence, it's help, it's heart. Thank you for all of the above, beautiful people in our lives. We have felt your love in our darkest moment and we feel truly blessed. Jack is doing better than we could ever have hoped and anyone who has seen how far he fell knows it's a miracle he is here with us today."*

Romans 8:28 says *'All things work together for good for those who love God.'* Note it doesn't say 'All things **are** good for those who love God.' It's important to acknowledge that hard times

will come your way… and you aren't expected to thank God ***for*** them. Especially while you're in the midst of it all.

But to be thankful ***in*** them, as 1 Thessalonians 8:13 suggests, is something else altogether.

When a friend came round a few weeks later and saw where Jack had fallen, she said: "Man, your God has been tough on you."

I looked at her, surprised: 'No, my God has been good to me.'

A while ago I shared my story and someone commented "of course you're grateful. Your son is alive." The anguish in her voice revealed an unspeakable loss. Only one who has experienced the tragic loss of a loved one has authority to speak into the heart of it.

Horatio G. Spafford was a successful lawyer from Chicago. He and his wife, Anne had five children together. In 1871, their young son died of pneumonia and their business was gravely impacted by the Chicago fire. In 1873, their four daughters drowned when the ship they were travelling on with Anne sank.

Anne was rescued and when she made it to shore, she wired Spafford a telegram that read: "Saved alone, what shall I do?" He later framed the telegram and hung it in his office.

Spafford took the next ship to meet his wife and wrote the timeless hymn [7]'It is Well With My Soul' as the ship sailed over the place where his daughters had drowned.

When peace like a river attendeth my way,

When sorrows like sea billows roll,

Whatever my lot, Thou hast taught me to say,

It is well, it is well with my soul.

Even in the most tragic circumstances, God can reach in and create something beautiful. Just ask my friend, Kara. Before she became a Christian, Kara was pretty much as far from God as you can get. This is her story…

Looking back, I realise my wild behaviour began after many years of being ostracised and even bullied at school. A friendless, unattractive 'nerd' from a low-income household, with very young parents who were really still kids themselves, I searched for my identity in falsehoods. Then, at 17 I suddenly 'bloomed' and I was thrust into a new world, finally accepted by the fun, popular crowd. I fell head over heels in love with a guy named Tommy. He was like no one I'd ever met before, or since. He was handsome, charismatic, and someone you just wanted to be around. We had a strange magnetic attraction and the day after we met, I told my best friend "I'm going to marry this guy." He tried to talk with me about starting a relationship but I was so immature, and broken, that I had no idea, not a clue, what a relationship was about. At 22, after he moved interstate, I moved about 45 minutes away from him. I had convinced myself that I was moving there for fun and not for him. Months went by and we were very reserved around each other, at his request. I gave it my best, but over time things got ugly.

He dated other girls, and I couldn't handle seeing that. We would get together and then I wouldn't hear from him. Although he was a bit of a lady's man, he had a kind heart and didn't want to hurt me. Eventually, he began to resent our strange relationship, as did I, and he said he hated me. That broke me. Everything I'd hoped for was spiralling into madness and I could not control it. I still hoped we might start over. One evening, I felt rather unsettled and couldn't shake it. Later that night something strange happened. I dreamt that something or someone told me Tommy was gone. As I opened my eyes, a friend came into my bedroom and told me the news that changed me forever... my Tommy had died in a car accident.

Fast forward a week, and I had cried bathtubs of tears, stopped eating, and was in an entirely different world, on my way to his funeral. I couldn't bring myself to peer into his open casket and see him one last time. I went to the back of the funeral home, and decided I needed to see some pictures of us together in the photo album that his family had put together. But as I skimmed through the pages, I realised that not one of the many pictures in the album included me. I had given all my photos to his family and not one of them made it into the album. It dawned on me that I was considered Tom's 'little thing on the side' to his new friends in this new town, and that I meant nothing to him. His family were not fond of me either, as we had gotten in some trouble together recently. So, this photo album really felt like they were making a statement, and I took it very hard. I thought that if I could just see us together in a photo, everything would be better. I stood up, walked over to his casket and tentatively looked at him. But what I saw took me by surprise. I suddenly knew that he wasn't there anymore but that he was *somewhere*. I was horrified and confused as I stared at his stillness. The person he was had left, and I was staring at his shell. Suddenly, I needed to know where he was.

A few hours and many drinks later, I was relieved to find that some friends from our hometown had come down for his funeral. It was so good to see some familiar faces. It was late when we all walked down to the beach. The stars were out, the moon was bright and it lit up the ocean we were now jumping in.

Eventually, everyone huddled together in the sand and cried and talked. I found a quiet spot and sat on the sand alone.

As I watched everyone chatting, I was drawn to the sky and noticed how beautiful it looked. I felt so incredibly sad.

More than sad, I was almost at the point of wanting to be done with life altogether. I couldn't imagine my life without him in it, and didn't *want* a life without him in it. I had truly believed I would eventually get it together and marry this man. That was all I wanted. And that hope was gone.

As I sat looking at the stars, I began speaking into the night, to someone I wasn't sure of. To this presence that I felt was looking after me. I said," I don't think I'm going to make it. I need to know if Tom even cared or loved me, or I think I'm going to die." And I meant it. My heart was more than broken. It was shattered. As I said the words, out of the corner of my eye, I saw someone get up and begin walking over to me. It was Tommy's best friend from back home, though I didn't know him too well. He came and stood beside me and said, "Kara, you know Tom cared about you, right?" I just looked at him, and as I did, he began to explain the reasons why he knew it, and shared Tom's most recent words about me that I didn't know about. Thoughtful words. I was bewildered. As he left, I thought, 'well, *that* was weird.' Before I had too much time to think, another of Tommy's close friends came over and said, "Kara, you know Tom loved you, right?" He also told me things Tom had said about me that he'd never told me himself. He shared stories about times that I never knew he spoke to anyone else about. Despite my incredible sadness, I felt a little spark of joy. Something was happening here.

This was the beginning of my understanding that God sees me. God showed me that he knew me before I even knew myself. I didn't turn to Jesus straight away, but I knew in that moment on the beach that there was something more. God delivered a life-saving message at exactly the right time, when my entire life felt ruined and wrong. He planted a first seed of hope. And that seed has been growing on fertile ground ever since. He healed my heart beyond anything I could ever imagine and blessed me with a wonderful husband and 2 beautiful children. I learned, and am still learning by His grace, what a relationship is about. In His mightiness and power, He even gave me a glimpse of hope for Tommy's soul. I found out months later that Tom believed in Jesus Christ as his saviour. And I know without a doubt that God is so very, very good.

I love King David's honesty with God and I think God loved it, too. After all, He calls David 'A man after His own heart.' David wasn't afraid to document his discontent and to cry out in anguish:

'How long, O Lord? Will you forget me forever? How long will you hide your face from me? How long must I take counsel in my soul and have sorrow in my heart all the day? How long shall my enemy be exalted over me?' Psalm 13:1-2

But his Psalms are also filled with words of thanks:

'Thank you! Everything in me says "Thank you!" Angels listen as I sing my thanks. I kneel in worship facing your holy temple and say it again: "Thank you!" Thank you for your love, thank you for your faithfulness; Most holy is your name, most holy is your Word. The moment I called out, you stepped in; you made my life large with strength.' Psalm 138:1-3

In 1 Chronicles 16:37-42 David even sets up a group of men with one job description: *"Give thanks to God, for his love never quits!"*

Whatever you're going through, the 'Father of rain and dew' has got this. His love never quits. Even in the tough times. Now ***that's*** something to be thankful for.

God would never ask me to thank Him for what happened to Jack. But I found ways to be thankful *in* it.

That first night in hospital, as I stared out at the city lights from my trundle bed, I thought about all the things I had to be thankful for in our darkest moment.

I was thankful for my neighbour who was there for me, no questions asked. For the ambulance officers who treated Jack on the way to hospital. For the team of Doctors and Nurses who gave him the highest level of care. For my mum who sat beside me for two days. For my sister-in-law who travelled two hours to help look after Tyson. And of course, I was so incredibly thankful that my Jack was alive… bruised and sore… but alive none-the-less. We would have a nervous three year wait until he started Kindergarten to see the full extent of any brain damage that might lead to learning difficulties. Today, he's a B grade student. No sign of brain damage.

It's easy to thank God when things are going well but what about when the going gets tough? Job was a man truly blessed by God – he had wealth, health, a wife and children. He praised God and lived a life that pleased Him. In Job 1:11 Satan talks to God about Job: *"But what do you think would happen if you reached down and took away everything that is his? He'd curse you right to your face, that's what."*

When his family, health and wealth, and most of his friends have been taken from him, Job finally cries out *'What have I done to deserve this?'* Job 30:24

And how does God respond?

"Have you ever travelled to where snow is made,
seen the vault where hail is stockpiled,
The arsenals of hail and snow that I keep in readiness
for times of trouble and battle and war?
Can you find your way to where lightning is launched,
or to the place from which the wind blows?
Who do you suppose carves canyons
for the downpours of rain, and charts
the route of thunderstorms
That bring water to unvisited fields,
deserts no one ever lays eyes on,
Drenching the useless wastelands
so they're carpeted with wildflowers and grass?
And who do you think is the father of rain and dew,
the mother of ice and frost?
You don't for a minute imagine
these marvels of weather just happen, do you?" Job 38:22-30

It's been [2]scientifically proven that grateful people are more resilient. I've certainly found that focussing on everything I had to be thankful for that night, rather than the horror of almost losing a child, has helped me move forward.

'One act of thanksgiving when things go wrong with us is worth a thousand thanks when things are agreeable to our inclination.' - St John of Avila (1500–1569)

Lipstick on Your Teeth

'LIFE'S SHORT. HAVE AN AFFAIR.' That was Ashley Maddison's catchphrase – a website dedicated to facilitating extra-marital affairs.

In 2015, hackers released the names of 30 million married Ashley Maddison account holders, who had registered with the website to solicit secret liaisons.

30 million people.

Just pause and think about that for a moment. That's 30 million married people who looked at their partners one day and thought, 'you're not enough for me. I deserve more.' And that's just those with the audacity to register their details on one particular website!

Of course, any married person who's completely honest will tell you that it's easy to find faults in our partners.

Abraham Lincoln said: "If you look for the bad in people expecting to find it, you surely will." The problem is that you don't even have to look for it, it's just there!

Much like the majestic Ibis, so regal as it soared across the skies, a distinctive pink line across its glorious wingspan, its noble black beak, pointing onwards, toward its exotic destination. Then the Ibis looked down upon the rubbish created by humans and saw that it was good. And that is how the once majestic Ibis became known as the lowly 'Bin Chicken.' Then humans saw that the distinctive pink line under its wings was just a vulnerable bald spot, matching the baldness on its head. Its once 'noble' beak became an annoyance, leering over unfinished sandwiches, still clutched by human hands and it no longer soared overhead toward exotic destinations, settling instead for public rubbish bins.

I'm certain that if I asked you right now to list 10 things that bother you about your erstwhile intriguing partner, you'd have no trouble at all… their snoring, driving style, dancing style, cooking style, table manners, messiness (or militant cleanliness), morning breath, temper or lack of affection. They're all 'top of mind,' right? Their air of mystery long dissipated.

Now list 10 things you're grateful for about your partner.

The longer you've been married, the longer it may take you to craft this list. All the things you loved about them before you said 'I do' may have become a distant memory. Blurred by time and seasons and the busyness of life.

Seeing the good in others takes practice and intentionality.

Or in the words of Anne Frank, "Dead people receive more flowers than the living ones because regret is stronger than gratitude."

A couple of years into our marriage, Phil decided to take up playing footy (AFL) again. He joined a local club and started training. In the leadup to their first match, the players went away on a team bonding 'footy trip.' This involved heading 'out bush,' sleeping in tents and drinking heavily around a campfire. On the first night, one of the young players had an idea. "Let's all share our best 'dirty weekend' stories." Phil hunched in his camp chair. There was no way to leave the campfire without appearing to be turning his back on his teammates. The whole weekend was about team building and this type of 'banter' was considered a normal part of footy culture. He sat in silence as young blokes regaled their teammates with tales of their most 'colourful' conquests, each story more vulgar than the last. Eventually, it was Phil's turn to share and he prayed quickly for wisdom. "You know what, fellas," he said, "the greatest joy in my life… is my wife. I'm so thankful for her." To his surprise, an awed silence descended over the campfire. Finally, one of his teammates spoke; "You're a lucky man, Phil," he said, and his teammates nodded in agreement. With one statement, Phil had transformed the atmosphere around the campfire, and the conversation quickly shifted to more positive subjects.

From that moment, whenever I came into the club, Phil's teammates treated me like royalty. They would often join us for a drink and ask me for relationship advice… Like where they could find a girl like me.

It became clear that despite their campfire bravado about all the girls they had casually bedded, what these young men really yearned for was a Proverbs 31 wife (although they had probably never read about her in the bible for themselves).

Phil could have complained to his teammates about my propensity for creating mess, or my lack of prowess in the kitchen. He could have told them about how my hair clogs the bathroom sink, or that I hate losing an argument. But his gratitude toward me had the power to change culture and mindsets amongst his teammates.

Shifting focus from the things that bother you about someone, to the things that make you smile brings a new perspective and appreciation. So, when you look at your partner, parent, or friend... what are you focussing on?

'Get along among yourselves, each of you doing your part. Our counsel is that you warn the freeloaders to get a move on. Gently encourage the stragglers, and reach out for the exhausted, pulling them to their feet. Be patient with each person, attentive to individual needs. And be careful that when you get on each other's nerves you don't snap at each other. ***Look for the best in each other, and always do your best to bring it out.****'* - 1 Thessalonians 5:15 (emphasis mine)

An important component in any healthy relationship is the ability to receive feedback and correction with gratitude. Yes, you can (and should) be thankful when you receive correction.

Every girl needs a friend who'll tell her when she has lipstick on her teeth; literally and metaphorically. There's nothing worse than getting home after a night out with friends only to look in the mirror and discover you've had lipstick on your teeth the whole time, or lettuce wedged between your incisors. Or worse, your fly is undone, or your skirt is tucked into your underpants, and no one told you!

Even more so when you realise you've been walking around with a personality flaw that no one's had the courage to mention.

The fact is, your loved ones may well love you enough to give you correction, but they might be fearful of telling you a hard truth about yourself because it will be met with an angry outburst, or stone-cold silence and so they watch you walk through life with proverbial lipstick on your teeth, and you miss out on becoming the very best person you *could* be.

There was a time during my senior year at high school, when I noticed a close friend becoming distant. She'd stopped returning my phone calls and didn't sit with our group for lunch any more. I asked someone why my friend had been avoiding me. Softly, she told me a hard truth about myself that I hadn't realised. She explained that my friend had been too frightened to tell me herself. "We're all a bit scared of your temper, to be honest," she said. I was incensed. "I do NOT have a bad temper!" I yelled, bristling with rage, then almost instantaneously experienced an 'aha' moment. My friends had been too frightened to tell me something I really needed to hear, and so I was missing out on becoming a better person. I worked hard at controlling my temper and learning to be grateful whenever someone I look up to chose to bless me with their honest feedback. After all, *'welcoming correction is a mark of good sense.'* Proverbs 15:5

Have you ever met someone suffering from the [3]Dunning-Kruger Effect? In short, it's the inability to recognise your own inability. Basically, it describes someone with low ability, who doesn't have the skills to recognise their incompetence, also known as a lack of self-awareness.

'The Dunning-Kruger Effect' was discovered by Cornell University psychologists David Dunning and Justin Kruger. During their study, participants were tested on logic, grammar, and sense of humour. What they found was that those who performed the worst, rated themselves well above average.

You'll find examples of The Dunning-Kruger Effect by watching outtake auditions for singing competitions. Each episode features tone deaf and overconfident would-be divas who fancy themselves the greatest undiscovered talent in the industry. I watched on in horror during an episode as one of the judges, gob-smacked by what he had just witnessed said, "Did no one love you enough to tell you that you have absolutely no singing talent whatsoever?" Indignant, the contestant replied, "My friends *love* my voice. They *encouraged* me to audition." I couldn't bear to watch any more.

'*Faithful are the wounds of a friend [who corrects out of love and concern].*' Proverbs 27:6 (AMP)

After graduating from high school, I studied Hospitality Management. I'd had a couple of after-school waitressing jobs and had visions of owning a restaurant. A few months in, during the 'kitchen skills' component of the course, I was hit with a hard truth. I struggled with gutting a chicken, I'll admit, and I tended to 'freestyle' recipes, with disastrous results, but I thought I was doing pretty well. A pep talk to the whole class from our Head Chef left me in no doubt that I was on the right track. "I know some of you feel like you're struggling," he said, "but I want to encourage you that you're all doing tremendously well, so don't be discouraged." That was the 'shot in the arm' I needed. I puffed out my chest and picked up my knife block, ready to walk back to my bench when the Head Chef signalled me over to his desk. "That speech I just gave everyone…" I nodded, smiling. "None of that was directed at you. You really are a terrible Chef." Ouch. That hurt. I had

Dunning-Krugered my career in hospitality. I cried angry tears and griped about his insensitivity but really, there was no point in sugar coating it. I really was a terrible Chef. And, on reflection, I really was a terrible waitress, too. So, I packed up my knife block and considered my options. I'm still a terrible 'Chef,' so my husband does most of the cooking at home (he happens to be a brilliant cook and the king of barbecue).

Of course, a big part of receiving feedback is ensuring you have the self-awareness to determine whether it has merit, or not. As Paul writes to Timothy: *'keep a close check on yourself. And don't worry too much about what the critics will say.'* (1 Timothy 5:22)

Do you want to know the opposite of the Dunning-Kruger Effect? It's 'Imposter Syndrome.' This is the condition that prevents so many people from stepping out into their destiny. They are so afraid that they might be suffering from the Dunning-Kruger Effect, they do nothing and all they've achieved is anonymity.

If Thomas Edison had convinced himself he was a sufferer of the Dunning-Kruger Effect after his 1,000th failed attempt at inventing the lightbulb, we would never have heard of him.

The difference between success and failure is a willingness to fail forward and accept constructive criticism.

Around the time my hubby rekindled his football career, I decided to give soccer another try. I found a local women's soccer club and attended training at the local park. I got on well with my teammates and I was quite enjoying myself. The coach was very good, but I noticed he really 'had a go' at some of the girls during training, pulling them up on their technique and pointing out minor mistakes. While others, like myself, didn't receive any feedback at all.

I naturally assumed this was because I was doing so well that there was nothing I needed to improve. However, the day of the first game was approaching and after training one night, the starting line-up was announced. To my surprise, the girls our coach had been harshest with all made the team, and one particular girl he'd really 'put under the pump' was named captain. Then, the penny dropped. He was targeting those girls with 'feedback' because he saw something in them that was worthwhile. He wanted them to improve because he knew they were capable of great things. They were 'team' material. And, despite my best efforts, I was not.

Hebrews 12:4-11 talks about discipline as a form of training: *'This trouble you're in isn't punishment; it's training,'* and likens His discipline to that of a parent. He knows we discipline our children because we love them and want them to be their absolute best selves. And that is no easy task!

Parenting expert Michelle Mitchell once said to me "parenting's only hard if you're doing it right." Amen to that! At the end of a long, hard day of shaping the lives of miniature humans, I'm often physically and emotionally exhausted. Parenting shouldn't feel like permanent jetlag, should it? I remember my mother saying to me right before handing down some 'discipline' when I was a little girl: "This hurts me more than it hurts you." I responded "well, don't do it, then!" Of course, she went ahead with my punishment anyway, because shaping me into a decent human being was more important than feeling comfortable.

God's 'discipline' is no different. *'My dear child, don't shrug off God's discipline, but don't be crushed by it either. It's the child he loves that he disciplines; the child he embraces, he also corrects. God is educating you; that's why you must never drop out.'* Hebrews 12:4-11

When an organisation dedicated to Prison Chaplaincy asked me to write a series of articles about ex-inmates, I wasn't sure what to expect.

Sitting down to my first interview, a fine-looking young man smiled at me from across the table.

"I don't know anything about you," I said, keeping a completely open mind. "Tell me, what were you in for?"

He squirmed in his seat for a moment, then looked at me earnestly. "First degree murder," he replied.

Suddenly, my survival instincts kicked in, my heart started racing and I found myself fighting the urge to jump up and run out of the room. 'Be cool' I thought, struggling to calm myself, hoping I'd managed to look completely unfrazzled. He told me his story of drug addiction and a drug deal gone wrong, but then there was a shift in the conversation. As he started to speak about encountering Jesus behind bars, his face began to glow. He spoke with such awe and gratitude as he recalled the moment that he realised that God loved him right there, in his prison cell, in his brokenness. He'd never felt so free as he kneeled on the hard floor and asked God for forgiveness. He spoke of God's kindness, putting him in prison so he could experience real love for the first time as he spoke with the Prison Chaplains. "There are millions of people on the outside, living in prisons they've built for themselves," he said. "But inside my prison cell, I felt truly free for the first time in my entire life."

Since that first interview, I've spoken with convicted murderers, drug dealers, armed robbers and violent criminals, who all did hard time and have a few of things in common…

1. Their faces light up as they speak about God's kindness.
2. They all found true freedom for the first time while reading their bible inside their prison cell, or at the weekly prison chapel service.
3. Their transformations are both undeniable and miraculous.
4. During their darkest season, the greatest work was being carried out.
5. They didn't shrug off God's discipline, or let it crush them. They embraced it, just as He embraced them.

Showing Up

It was an evening I'll never forget. One of my dear friends had booked out a private room in our city's swankiest restaurant to celebrate her birthday. The invitation mentioned something about dressing up, leaving kids at home, and enjoying an evening of decadent fine dining, accompanied by exquisite wines and waterfront views. To say I was bristling with excitement would have been an understatement.

As I sank into a sumptuously cushioned chair, clutching my first glass of wine and gazing in wonder at the river through floor-to-ceiling windows, I felt overwhelmed with gratitude at the pleasure of the experience.

But as the entree was carefully placed before us by impeccably dressed waiters, one of the guests pointed to an empty chair. Someone was missing.

That 'someone,' we were informed, had RSVP'd their attendance but for reasons known only to themselves, had failed to show up.

I was dumbfounded. Knowing the glorious evening that lay ahead of us, what could possibly have been more important? Could you *really* just 'forget' your friend's lavish birthday party? Apparently, you could.

I looked down at the plate of food before me (more a work of art than an entree, really), and observed every detail. Each item had been carefully placed just so, then festooned with strategically scattered edible flower petals.

It almost felt sacrilegious dipping my fork into a corner and tearing away a morsel. As I gently placed the fragrant offering into my mouth, I imagined this might be very much what heaven will be like. I closed my eyes, as you do when experiencing something truly transcendent, opening them only when distracted by movement beside me. My dining neighbour was beaming at me. "Have you ever tasted something so amazing, you just feel like crying with pure joy?" she whispered. Yes. Yes I have. Right in this moment.

The conversation once again turned to the missing guest. How could they forget? What had kept them away? Why didn't they let anyone know? How rude! If only they knew what they were missing.

"I would never RSVP and not show up." Someone around the table said, indignant. We all agreed. It would just never happen. Not to me.

The next morning, I was tidying my desk, as I do once every year or so, and there it was, underneath a baseball cap, a bottle of multi-vitamins and a handmade bowl my son had lovingly crafted at school. An invitation. For an event yesterday morning. One I had RSVP'd to and then promptly forgot about.

I was mortified. Horrified. Embarrassed. Ashamed. I had committed the ultimate social faux pas. I was a 'no show.' I immediately called the host and apologised profusely. I knew it was bad. She had prepaid my meal. There was a chair with my name on it. People were expecting me, and I was at home, in my pyjamas, completely oblivious. She was very gracious. "These things happen," she said. 'Not to me,' I thought. 'I'm not that person who doesn't show up.' But apparently, I am.

Luke 14:15-24 describes a similar scene. A man throws a generous dinner party, but all his invitees have 'better' things to do. They don't realise what they're missing out on. All they had to do was show up. *'How fortunate the one who gets to eat dinner in God's kingdom!'*

The grateful life means not just accepting God's invitation to the celebration feast, it means actually showing up.

And what does 'showing up' look like?

'So here's what I want you to do, God helping you: Take your everyday, ordinary life—your sleeping, eating, going-to-work, and walking-around life—and place it before God as an offering. Embracing what God does for you is the best thing you can do for him. Don't become so well-adjusted to your culture that you fit into it without even thinking. Instead, fix your attention on God. You'll be changed from the inside out. Readily recognize what he wants from you, and quickly respond to it. Unlike the culture around you, always dragging you down to its level of immaturity, God brings the best out of you, develops well-formed maturity in you.' Romans 12:1-2

A grateful life is spent in perpetual delight (Psalm 37:4). Living each day immersed in His presence, focussed on His goodness, and delighted in finding new ways to 'pay forward' His gifts.

It means 'showing up' even when you'd rather stay home (metaphorically speaking). Because a grateful life shines bright, like a city on a hill. If no one around you could guess that you're a Christian, check your glow.

'You're here to be light, bringing out the God-colours in the world. God is not a secret to be kept. We're going public with this, as public as a city on a hill. If I make you light-bearers, you don't think I'm going to hide you under a bucket, do you? I'm putting you on a light stand. Now that I've put you there on a hilltop, on a light stand—shine! Keep open house; be generous with your lives. By opening up to others, you'll prompt people to open up with God, this generous Father in heaven.' Matthew 5:14-16

'Showing up' means choosing joy, even when the tough times come (notice I said 'when' and not 'if'), because a grateful life believes that God is good all the time.

'Be cheerful no matter what; pray all the time; thank God no matter what happens. This is the way God wants you who belong to Christ Jesus to live.' 1 Thessalonians 5:18

'Showing up' means putting others first, even if it means missing out.

In 2020, the world was gripped by the COVID-19 pandemic, It also came to be known as 'Great Toilet Paper Crisis.' You may not read about it in history books, but everyone who lived through it will never forget. A highly contagious virus was spreading throughout the world, and the media had whipped the public into a frenzy as nations closed their borders and we were all told to 'self-isolate' as best we could. What followed was weeks of 'panic buying.' Regular, otherwise 'normal' people were coming to fisticuffs over toilet paper and hand sanitiser in supermarket aisles, despite assurances that these products were not in short supply. Grocery stores were forced to employ security staff to guard their stocks of 3 ply and essentials were rationed at the checkout, as manufacturers struggled to keep up with demand.

'Seniors Only' shopping hours were introduced because the elderly just couldn't compete with the young and terrified panic buyers, who had stuffed their trolleys to overflowing with non-perishables, leaving empty shelves in their wake.

One global pandemic revealed the true heart of mankind and it was ugly.

But it was a time for believers to shine.

Our local church delivered food parcels and even toilet paper to the needy, which included many who had been doing just fine before the pandemic hit, but who found themselves unemployed due to business closures.

It's not the first time Christians have 'shown up' during a pandemic.

During the Spanish Influenza Pandemic of 1919, at a time before women even had the right to vote, God spoke to Aimee Semple McPherson and told her to stop in Tulsa on her way home to Los Angeles. Her act of obedience in the face of fear ignited a revival.

She defied the local ban on church gatherings and believed that God could heal all those who were suffering.

She drove around in her 'Gospel Car' and ministered to victims of the epidemic, leaving miraculous healings in her wake.

Christians have a long history of 'showing up' during times of crisis but we don't always get it right.

A famous study called 'The Darley-Batson Good Samaritan Experiment[4],' which was conducted at Princeton University in the 1970s, highlighted our human nature.

The subjects of the study were Divinity Students, who were asked to write and present a sermon on The Good Samaritan, found in Luke 10:25-37.

Participants then had to walk to another building to meet another member of the team before delivering their sermon.

Here, the team member told each participant one of three things:

A. They were early and had plenty of time.
B. They were on-time but should head over straight away to avoid being late.
C. They were late and really needed to hurry if they were going to make it.

Then the next part of the study came into play. Another team member faked a sudden illness, collapsing on the floor in the narrow hallway, blocking the way to the room where the students would be presenting their sermon. The would-be Priests had to step over the fallen stranger in order to get into the room. The results of the study were very confronting.

63% of participants who had been told they were 'early' stopped to help the stranger.

45% of participants who had been told they were 'on time' stopped to help the stranger.

And a lowly 10% of participants who had been told they were 'late' stopped to help the stranger.

These are people with the very best of intentions. Priests-in-the-making who had just written a sermon about helping a stranger, but when they were faced with the scenario in real life, very few 'showed up.'

I'm sure 100% of the participants in this study would have said, without hesitation, that they would have stopped to help a stranger, regardless of how much time they had. But good intentions and lived experience are two different things.

I don't think anyone on January 1, 2020 pictured themselves fighting over toilet paper, but I watched it happen time and time again on the news. Our sense of 'self-preservation' is so intrinsic to our fallen nature, it takes 'dying to ourselves' to deny our survival instincts and truly put others first.

'If you've gotten anything at all out of following Christ, if his love has made any difference in your life, if being in a community of the Spirit means anything to you, if you have a heart, if you care —then do me a favour: Agree with each other, love each other, be deep-spirited friends. Don't push your way to the front; don't sweet-talk your way to the top. Put yourself aside, and help others get ahead. Don't be obsessed with getting your own advantage. Forget yourselves long enough to lend a helping hand.' Philippians 2:3

Years ago, when my friend Pam was a young working mum, she was feeling quite stretched and time-poor. Her sister-in-law, who at the time was not terribly interested in Christian things, called Pam with the news that her mother-in-law was in hospital, terminally ill and she asked Pam if she would mind visiting and praying for her on her deathbed.

Despite all the busy-ness around her, Pam dropped everything and showed up. On arrival, the woman was unresponsive, and her carer was sitting beside her bed, keeping vigil. Pam chatted with her for a while, with no response, and then announced that she was going to pray. As Pam prayed, she included a bit of the Sinners Prayer, as she had been told that the patient had never experienced a relationship with the Lord and feared for her future. When Pam said "Amen," the woman opened her eyes and looked at Pam with such intensity she will never forget it. Pam had a sense that she was standing on hallowed ground. That this woman's life had changed in that moment, and she was trying to convey that to Pam but didn't have the capacity to speak. She was never able to speak again and died later that day. Pam is forever grateful to have that experience etched in her memory… the intensity of her eyes, trying to convey so much in a look. Pam believes that she realised for the first time in her life, at death's door, that she needed a saviour. God's timing is perfect, and Pam was so glad that she had made herself available to present Him to her in her helplessness and hopelessness.

Christians should be the 'feet washers' of the world, just as Jesus washed the feet of his disciples (John 13:1-17). It's not glamorous or celebrated. It's dirty work with little, or no reward this side of heaven. And it's often very humbling.

In my early 20s, I volunteered at a Holiday Mission in Cowra, a small town in Central West New South Wales. I'd never been on a mission trip before but I loved being part of our kids ministry at church, so I thought this would be a fun week away, sharing the gospel with kids.

I made friends with another volunteer during the pre-mission training sessions and we decided to drive to Cowra together. We laughed and chatted, sharing our expectations. We hadn't really thought about accommodation but assumed we would be billeted out to family homes in the community.

We arrived a Cowra Showgrounds, where the mission was being held, for our induction and we noticed a large section of the hall had been curtained off and blow-up mattresses in situ. "We're not sleeping in here, are we?" my friend asked, her voice wavering. "Oh no," replied one of the mission leaders, "we wouldn't put the girls in here! This is the boys' sleeping quarters." Phew! We were so relieved. Sleeping on the timber floor in an old hall just seemed so undignified.

Following our induction, one of the leaders announced they would guide us to our accommodation. Brandishing a torch, she lead us across a grassy field. We weren't getting into a car and heading to a local family's home, then? We started to feel nervous. Soon, we could hear girls' voices through the darkness as we approached a horse shed, with tarpaulins draped over doorways and window frames, barnyard smells emanating from within.

"Here you are," our guide announced. We both froze, speechless. "We're sleeping.... *here*?" I asked, my voice shaking. "In the... horse sheds?" Yes. In the horse sheds.

My friend and I looked at each other, horrified. We'd both missed the memo about sleeping arrangements. We were city girls, with nothing but high heels and dresses in our bags. This was not even close to what we were expecting.

A group of girls helped us blow up borrowed mattresses and laid them side-by-side in our designated stall. We both cried a little bit and tried to get comfortable. Just as I was dozing off, a shriek rang out through the shed and every girl sat bolt upright in our sleeping bags. The shrieker cried; "A rat just ran across my pillow!" I don't think we slept more than 2 hours the whole week.

Each morning, my friend and I would roll toward each other, bleary eyed, and announce the countdown: "Six days to go!" We were so emotionally unprepared for the small sacrifice that had been asked of us. It took every ounce of willpower to put on a smile and be 'present' with the bright-eyed kids who showed up each day to hear about Jesus. But we pulled ourselves together and cheered each other on as we offered up our 'sacrifice of praise.' Christians all over the world who are persecuted for their faith would surely have rolled their eyes at our shallow protestations. Had I known what awaited us beforehand, would I have 'shown up' for the short-term mission? Probably not. And I would have missed an incredible opportunity to experience God's goodness as we loved on these dear children.

A few years later, I had grown in maturity and faith and I decided to try short term missions again. This time fully prepared for what that meant.

So, I signed up for a Beach Mission in Kingscliff - a sleepy coastal town in New South Wales.

We were accommodated in large tents on the local church property. We slept in bunks made from hessian sacks. This time, I was no shrinking violet, and I embraced the 'rough' sleeping conditions. One night I was awoken by a scared voice whispering, "help me!" I looked up to see the face of the girl above me and heard tearing as the hessian sack ripped under her weight. I got out of the way just in time before she unceremoniously plopped onto my bed below. I laughed hysterically as I helped her up and set up a makeshift bed on the floor for her. At the end of the mission, I was given the 'Happy Camper' award. What a difference a change in expectation makes!

I even came wearing a brand new pair of sandals, leaving my high heels at home.

However, these sandals needed some 'wearing in' and soon my feet were a blistery mess. By day five, the blisters were oozing pus and I was hobbling around in pain. I refused to let it dampen my spirits and I had a wonderful time, sharing Jesus with the kids. Until one morning, our camp leaders decided to do a team-building exercise with us. Half our team was asked to stand while the rest of us remained seated, myself included. The leaders brought in buckets of water and announced that those who were standing were to wash the feet of those who were sitting. I sat frozen, looking down at my pus-oozing dirty feet and shook my head. "No, I won't participate," I said. I couldn't ask someone to wash my feet and I didn't want to face the humiliation of watching each 'foot washer' walk by me, repulsed by what they saw.

But the team leaders insisted I remain seated and so I obeyed, heart racing, as 'feet washers' passed me by, my shame and embarrassment growing until I felt I would sink into the wooden floor beneath my chair. Until one lovely girl knelt in front of me and took my foot in her hand. "No!" I recoiled, pulling it back. "It's my honour to wash your feet," she said.

And so I sat still, tears rolling down my cheeks as she gently washed my indescribably awful feet with such humility and grace. My shame and embarrassment disappeared into the water with each gentle stroke of her hand. She personified 'showing up.'

I've volunteered on a number of short-term missions since. I've slept in wet sheets inside a leaky tent, danced in mud and cried with broken people as they shared their stories. I've learnt to show up and love every minute of it.

Of course, showing up doesn't have to mean going on a mission trip. You can 'show up' at your local grocery store. Let me explain…

Each year, our family goes away for a weekend with two other families. It started before we all had kids. We used to stay up late playing cards and watching movies, sleeping in, and eating decadent brunches. But that all changed once we started having children. Instead of playing cards, we stayed up nursing our little ones by night and chasing them around the coastal apartment by day, ensuring they didn't break anything, or hurt themselves. In short, we were exhausted.

So, early one morning I found myself at the nearby corner store, restocking our milk supplies to get us through the day. I felt jet lagged and not quite 'present.' The girl behind the counter was clearly a morning person (I am not, even at the best of times) and she was chattering away to me while I perused the dairy section. "I feel like I want to eat one of those donuts," she said, pointing to the baked goods behind a wall of glass. "Go for it!" I said, half-heartedly. "Yeah, but see I have this eating disorder" she replied, "and I have a really unhealthy relationship with food." I blinked. "Oh," I said.

She went on to tell me about her struggles with mental health and how she'd used food to self-medicate. I blinked again. A voice in my head started getting louder and louder, saying over and over again, 'tell her she needs Jesus. Tell her she needs Jesus.' 'I'm not saying that! She'll think I'm mad!' This battle raged inside my pre-caffeinated mind while this girl standing behind the counter continued to pour out her heart. Finally, I gave in. "You know what," I said, nearly vomiting out the words. I couldn't believe I was actually saying this in a corner store. "I think you need Jesus." She paused. Mouth open for a moment. "You know what?" She said. "I think I do." So, there in a corner store, carton of milk in one hand and sleep on my mind, I shared the gospel with the girl behind the counter. I'll never know the impact of that conversation on her life but it certainly impacted mine. The call to 'show up' can come anywhere, any time. When you're least prepared and when it's least convenient. Show up anyway.

One morning, I received an email from our boys' school to say that a much loved student was unconscious, following a car accident. I didn't know the girl, but my heart was broken for everyone who did. A group of mums gathered in the car park to pray as her life support was switched off. Our heartbroken, tear-soaked prayers were for her family, her friends and the school community. We prayed that God would use this tragedy to bring about revival in our school. I felt God put Psalm 27:13 on my heart as a promise *'I remain confident of this: I will see the goodness of the Lord in the land of the living.'* (NIV)

A few days later, I drove past the scene of the crash, which had been turned into a shrine. A cross was nailed to the light post where the car had struck, and flowers were lovingly placed on the grass beneath. Teenagers were milling around in a silent vigil. Comforting each other and standing close. I wished there were something I could do. 'They don't want a random mum hanging around,' I thought, as I continued driving. A couple of weeks later, our School Chaplain told me how thankful she was to one of the men in our church. He too had driven past the scene of the crash and witnessed the mourning teens. But he didn't just *wish* there were something he could do. He stopped at the local coffee shop and bought hot chocolates for each teen, then parked his car nearby and walked over to present his warm offering. He stood with them and prayed with them. He listened to them and comforted them. Touched by his act of kindness, some of those teens had started coming to our church. I was so happy to hear that but at the same time, I couldn't help but to think about those Theology students I spoke about earlier, and how like them I had been as I drove past the scene without stopping. Although I wasn't in a hurry to preach a sermon about the Good Samaritan, I was worried about what they might think of me. But one man from our church thought like Paul in 1 Corinthians 4:1-4, saying to himself, *'I don't care what anyone thinks of me. I don't even care what I think of myself. I only care what God thinks of me and I'll do whatever He wants me to do.'* That is the essence of 'showing up.'

And sometimes 'showing up' means standing alone. Just ask Daniel as he stood alone in the lion's den. Or Shadrach, Meshach, and Abednego, who stood in defiance, while everyone around them fell to their knees.

As part of her military training, my friend Jesse was required to take part in a Personal Development course. On the first morning, she sat with the other students, listening to the instructor explain what was ahead of them. Her eyes widened as he announced that they would be doing yoga and hypnosis. She had a strong conviction about the spiritual nature of these practices and couldn't stand before God with a clear conscience if she participated. But she was also painfully aware that failing to complete each component of the course could impact her ability to graduate and she could face disciplinary action as a consequence of her disobedience.

But her love for God was greater than her fear. She took comfort in the story of Shadrack, Meshack and Abednego. All they had to do was bow to the King in order to avoid death by raging fire. They chose the fire. But God didn't leave them in the fire alone. His angel was with them the whole time and they were covered by his protection, walking out unscathed.

Jesse explained to the instructor why she couldn't participate, and he heckled her throughout the morning. "We're just doing the moves," he said, "It's not spiritual."

God gave her a vision and she said, "If I use a knife to turn a screw, does it become a screwdriver, or does it remain a knife?"

Her request to be excused went up the chain of command, each one not knowing quite what to do about it. Finally, the day of the first yoga session arrived and she was told to speak with the yoga instructor herself. She explained respectfully why she couldn't, in good conscience, participate in a spiritual practice that was an act of worship to anyone but her God. Then she waited in nervous silence for the instructor's response.

"You know what?" She said, "I really admire your courage." And that was that. Jesse was so comforted to have felt God's presence in the fire with her and relieved that she was able to remain steadfast in her convictions.

Grateful Giving

'REDEEM EVERY FIRSTBORN CHILD AMONG *your sons. When the time comes and your son asks you, 'What does this mean?' you tell him, 'God brought us out of Egypt, out of a house of slavery, with a powerful hand. When Pharaoh stubbornly refused to let us go, God killed every firstborn in Egypt, the firstborn of both humans and animals. That's why I make a sacrifice for every first male birth from the womb to God and redeem every firstborn son.' The observance functions like a sign on your hands or a symbol on the middle of your forehead: God brought us out of Egypt with a powerful hand.'* Exodus 13:14-16 (Redeeming your first-born son meant paying 5 shekels to the Priest. Jesus' parents honoured this tradition in Luke 2:27)

It was a casual Sunday afternoon, and we were relaxing on our neighbour's deck, the aromas of barbeque and freshly mown grass lingering in the air, when someone asked me a question I'd never really pondered before… "You go to church, right? Can you tell me why churches are always asking for money?"

I paused for a moment, considering my response. "Well, what kind of Christian would I be if I *didn't* give? And what kind of church doesn't remind its people to live generously?"

That's exactly what Exodus 13:14-16 is saying - Remind yourself of what God has given you, by giving of yourself. It's the ultimate expression of gratitude.

In the words of Isaac Watts:

[5]*When I survey the wondrous cross*
on which the Prince of Glory died;
my richest gain I count but loss,
and pour contempt on all my pride.

Forbid it, Lord, that I should boast,
save in the death of Christ, my God;
all the vain things that charm me most,
I sacrifice them to his blood.

See, from his head, his hands, his feet,
sorrow and love flow mingled down.
Did e'er such love and sorrow meet,
or thorns compose so rich a crown.

Were the whole realm of nature mine,
that were an offering far too small;
love so amazing, so divine,
demands my soul, my life, my all.

Truly comprehending God's goodness compels us to express our gratitude through generosity. Paying forward the kindness He has shown to us is a gift in and of itself. As Jesus said, *'you're far happier giving than getting.'* Acts 20:35

So, what does 'grateful giving' look like?

*'Cain brought an offering to God from the produce of his farm. Abel also brought an offering, but **from the firstborn animals of his herd, choice cuts of meat**. God liked Abel and his offering, but Cain and his offering didn't get his approval. Cain lost his temper and went into a sulk.'* Genesis 4:3-5 (emphasise mine).

It's important to understand that these offerings were made before the rules surrounding offerings had even been set. It wouldn't be until the book of Leviticus that types of sacrifices would be stipulated. So, without any rules, how were they to know what would please God?

Quite simply, their offerings showed the content of their hearts. It wasn't about following rules. Abel gave his best (firstborn), while Cain kept his first fruits for himself. In giving his best, Abel was reflecting God's blessings that he enjoyed. Cain's response to God's disapproval revealed that he just didn't get it: *'Cain lost his temper and went into a sulk.'* He later killed his own brother, thinking that with Abel out of the way, he might find contentment with God and we all know how *that* turned out…. (SPOILER ALERT: endless wandering).

King David (a man after God's own heart) *really* got it. After an incredible display of compassion from God, David told Araunah he wanted to make an offering on his threshing floor. Araunah responds: *"Look, here's an ox for the burnt offering and threshing paddles for the fuel and wheat for the meal offering—it's all yours!"* David replied to Araunah, *"No. I'm buying it from you, and at the full market price. I'm not going to offer God sacrifices that are no sacrifice." So, David bought the place from Araunah for six hundred shekels of gold. He built an altar to God there and sacrificed Whole-Burnt-Offerings and Peace-Offerings.'* 1 Chronicles 21:22-27

Thankfully, animal sacrifices are no longer required as an outward expression of the gratitude we feel in our hearts. A generous, grateful life (Romans 12:1-2) and our praise (Hebrew 13:15) are acceptable offerings.

A few dollars in the offering plate, given joyfully (2 Corinthians 9:7) is a modern day *'sign on your hands or symbol on the middle of your forehead.'* And it's a simple way to live out God's definition of a true believer as one who will *'... reach out to the homeless and loveless in their plight.'* James 1:27

What we give to God out of our wealth reflects the level of gratitude in our hearts. Like the poor widow who gave 2 cents at the temple, while others gave much more. Jesus pointed out that *'all the others gave what they'll never miss; she gave extravagantly what she couldn't afford—she gave her all.'* Mark 12:41-44

Too many Christians believe they are reservoirs of wealth, rather than conduits. It's not just for our own benefit that we're blessed. Taking care of the needs of others is a simple way of 'paying forward' God's generosity in our own lives. And it doesn't need to be grand or extravagant.

'Real religion, the kind that passes muster before God the Father, is this: Reach out to the homeless and loveless in their plight, and guard against corruption from the godless world.' James 1:27

Marta lived in Mozambique for a number of years and has many miraculous stories to share. This is one of them…

Walking through a village one day, her eyes were drawn to a little girl. She felt God say to her that this girl had never been able to speak, and He wanted to heal her. He instructed Marta to give the little girl the bottle of water she was holding.

In these villages, clean water is like liquid gold and children would always run up to Marta, mouths open in anticipation, asking for a sip, but this little girl wasn't able to ask.

Marta knelt in front of her and handed her the bottle of water. The little girl took a sip and to the astonishment of everyone around her, she began to speak!

One small act of kindness transformed the life of a little girl and the elders in the village declared that she had been healed by the Word of God!

[7]Researchers from the Max Planck Institute for Ornithology in Germany conducted an experiment with African grey parrots. The parrots had been trained to trade tokens for a food treat through an exchange window.

Then the exchange window was closed on one bird's cage, so that bird couldn't trade their pile of tokens. While its neighbour had an open exchange window but no tokens.

What happened next was extraordinary! The bird with the tokens passed them all to the tokenless bird, beak-to-beak, watching their companion exchange the token for a walnut reward repeatedly, until they had given all their tokens.

When the roles were reversed, the same exchange took place between the birds.

This simple act of generosity came so naturally for African grey parrots, and they all benefited from helping each other.

We humans can learn a thing or two from their unprompted kindness.

One morning, I was heading out to Play Group, and Jack was wearing the last clean nappy. I had foolishly promised to provide morning tea.

A last-minute trip to the grocery store used to be a breeze… before I had kids. But with little ones, it was like walking around with a time-bomb that could explode at any given moment.

On arrival, I unbuckled my boys from their car seats with promises of a chocolate milk if they were on their absolute very best behaviour, then we raced in. I shook off the nagging feeling that I'd forgotten something.

The boys *were* on their best behaviour. And I was pretty sure I'd managed to get everything on the list.

Cupcakes – check
Nappies – check
Chocolate milks – check
Ooooh, a new mascara. Why not?

The boys helped me load everything onto the conveyor belt at the register and the cashier scanned each item.

"How would you like to pay for that?" she smiled.

"Credit…." I smiled back, opening my wallet and…

'Oh no no no no no no no no no no!' Suddenly my memory returned with crystal clarity. I'd put my credit card into a different bag the night before.

Tears of frustration pricked my eyes. I couldn't believe it.

"I'm so sorry, I've wasted your time," I apologised to the cashier.

"Can I open my chocolate milk now?" Tyson asked joyfully. My shoulders slumped.

Then, out of the 'express lane' crowd came a kind voice; "I'll pay."

The crowd parted like the Red Sea before Moses, revealing an elderly gentleman with a gentle smile.

"I'll pay…" he said again, pulling cash from his wallet.

"Oh no, I couldn't…" I responded. Don't cry. Don't cry. Don't cry.

"How much is it?" He asked.

"Ah… $29.95."

"Well, I've got $30 here." He said, handing it over.

The cashier started putting my groceries back into their bags.

"I'll just leave my groceries here," he said to the cashier, handing over his items. "I've got to pop home and get some more cash."

The magnitude of what had just happened overwhelmed me as we raced back to the car.

Sitting in his car seat, sipping on his chocolate milk, Tyson paused thoughtfully and said, "that was really incredible what that man did, wasn't it mummy?"

"It really was," I replied. "Incredible."

After Play Group, I headed home to retrieve my credit card. Then drove back to the grocery store to purchase an offering of 'thanks' for the generous gentleman, to accompany the $30 cash I had put into an envelope.

I dropped into his house brandishing chocolates. He was very appreciative of the gesture. "I was in big trouble when I got home." He said. "My wife had sent me to the shops to buy flour so she could make biscuits for the grandkids and I returned empty handed, asking for more money." His wife nodded, bemused. He had given 'everything' in that moment, to fulfil my need and his sacrifice will never be forgotten.

How much greater Christ's sacrifice for us? A box of chocolates or a bottle of water doesn't quite cover a gift that grand, but a simple act of generosity, an offering of 'thanks' each day, can have a huge impact on the world around us for good and for God.

There are numerous stories throughout the bible of how a small act of generosity was turned into an great miracle.

John 6 documents the time Jesus turns five loves of bread and two fish, offered up by a young boy, into a feast for 5,000 people. And 1 Kings 17 tells the story of a widow who is gathering sticks to bake bread with the last of her supplies, yet she agrees to feed Elijah. As a result, her flour and oil don't run out until rain returns and Elijah even heals her son from the clutches of death.

'This most generous God who gives seed to the farmer that becomes bread for your meals is more than extravagant with you. He gives you something you can then give away, which grows into full-formed lives, robust in God, wealthy in every way, so that you can be generous in every way, producing with us great praise to God.' 2 Corinthians 9:11

Divine Forgiveness

'To err is human, to *forgive divine.*' Alexander Pope

There's a generosity of spirit that comes from truly understanding what has been given to you… and at what cost.

It's a lesson I learnt one lazy Sunday afternoon when Phil and I took our boys for a walk along the beach. Before we headed home, we decided to stop in at a little café to share some afternoon tea. We intentionally sat outside, thinking that would minimise the potential damage two unpredictable toddlers could incur.

The café's menu had been handwritten in lipstick on a full-length mirror that leaned delicately against the wall. By the time I spotted Tyson crawling behind it ('it's a tunnel, mummy!'), it was all too late. The lipstick frosted glass crashed unceremoniously to the ground, and shattered glass crackled under my feet as I lunged forward and grabbed Tyson, unharmed, from amongst the debris.

I was horrified and embarrassed. It was like one of those movie scenes where the band stops playing as everyone pauses, mid conversation, to turn and stare in bewilderment (and judgement) at the scene of a heinous crime.

The owner of the café; a tall, dark haired woman, quietly picked up a dustpan and broom and made her way over to the mess.

'I'm so sorry!' I blurted out, humiliated. 'Please tell me how much the mirror cost and I'll pay you for it right now!'

She glanced over her shoulder as she swept the shards of glass into the dustpan.

"Let me tell you a story," she said, calmly. "Last weekend, I took my five year old daughter out for dinner to a fancy restaurant with my husband and before we'd even sat down, she broke a very expensive lamp. I couldn't afford to pay for a replacement, but the restaurant owner was so kind. He didn't charge us for a new lamp. Not a cent! How can I charge you for an old mirror I bought at an op shop, when I've been shown mercy like that?"

That's grace personified right there! That's what 'paying it forward' looks like in real life.

If only the unforgiving debtor in Matthew 18:23-35 had understood this concept. He owed the king millions of dollars he could never hope to repay in his lifetime. The king *'ordered that he be sold—along with his wife, his children, and everything he owned—to pay the debt.'* But in an act of inexplicable mercy, the king had compassion on the man and released him of his unpayable debt.

But then, this same guy runs into a friend who owes him a few thousand dollars and promptly throws him into prison.

Is it any wonder that when the king gets wind of this, he throws the ungrateful servant into jail, too? The king's generosity was wasted on this man. He really didn't understand the fullness of what had been done for him.

There's an old saying that goes: Forgiveness is like releasing someone from prison and then realising you were the prisoner all along.

Divine Forgiveness looks like the father of the Prodigal Son (Luke 15:11-32), who didn't even wait for an apology! *'When he was still a long way off, his father saw him. His heart pounding, he ran out, embraced him, and kissed him. The son started his speech: 'Father, I've sinned against God, I've sinned before you; I don't deserve to be called your son ever again.'*

'But the father wasn't listening. He was calling to the servants, 'Quick. Bring a clean set of clothes and dress him. Put the family ring on his finger and sandals on his feet. Then get a grain-fed heifer and roast it. We're going to feast! We're going to have a wonderful time! My son is here—given up for dead and now alive! Given up for lost and now found!' And they began to have a wonderful time.'

And how about Esau? If there's anyone in the Bible who has a right to feel ticked off, it's poor old Esau. His brother stole his birthright and then ran away. He *was* angry for a while. But time gives way to perspective. When they were reunited, Jacob was terrified. He sent everyone up ahead, like a human shield but he needn't have worried. *'Esau ran up and embraced him, held him tight and kissed him. And they both wept.'* Genesis 33:4. That's the grace of a man who truly understands what he's been given by God.

Forgiveness doesn't come naturally – it's purely supernatural.

If you think you're tracking okay in this area, it's time to take the Forgiveness Test in Matthew 5:43-47.

'You're familiar with the old written law, 'Love your friend,' and its unwritten companion, 'Hate your enemy.'

'I'm challenging that. I'm telling you to love your enemies. Let them bring out the best in you, not the worst. When someone gives you a hard time, respond with the energies of prayer, for then you are working out of your true selves, your God-created selves.'

'This is what God does. He gives his best—the sun to warm and the rain to nourish—to everyone, regardless: the good and bad, the nice and nasty.

'If all you do is love the lovable, do you expect a bonus? Anybody can do that. If you simply say hello to those who greet you, do you expect a medal? Any run-of-the-mill sinner does that.' Matthew 5:43-47 (emphasis mine).

When The Lord's Prayer declares *'Forgive us our sins as we forgive those who sin against us,'* that's exactly what it means. Our forgiveness is an expression of our gratitude toward God for releasing us from our own unpayable debt. If you can't forgive someone, have you really grasped just how much you've been forgiven? This is amazing grace. What a gift!

Corrie Ten Boom and her family hid Jews in their home during WWII. As a result, they found themselves in a Concentration Camp. Corrie and her sister Betsy were stripped naked and as she stood in her shame and humiliation, she thought of Jesus naked on the cross bearing her sins. The conditions were unimageable – lice infested lodgings, back breaking labour and merciless cruelty marked their days. Betsy died before she tasted freedom. Years later, Corrie Ten Boom was speaking at an event in Berlin and afterwards she was approached by a man she recognised immediately as one of the cruellest of the Nazis in their concentration camp.

He said he had encountered Jesus and he knew his sins were forgiven. He had asked Jesus for the opportunity to see one of his victims so he could ask for their forgiveness, too. Corrie looked him in the eye, and she was filled with nothing but hatred and unforgiveness. But then she recalled the Lord's prayer and its command to forgive.

She cried out to God for help and suddenly Romans 5:5 came to mind; *'we can't round up enough containers to hold everything God generously pours into our lives through the Holy Spirit.'*

She said, "Thank you God that your love is stronger than my hatred and unforgiveness." That same moment she was free.

Corrie held out her hand and she recalls, *"it was as if I felt God's love stream through my arms. You've never touched so, the ocean of God's love, as that you forgive your enemies.*

"Can you forgive?

No.

I can't either.

But He can."

The Antidote to Fear

'So we fix our eyes not on what is seen, but on what is unseen, since what is seen is temporary, but what is unseen is eternal.'
2 Corinthians 4:18

It was a dark and stormy night when Josh got into his car. It was very late, and he was weary. He drove toward home along winding roads, rain pelting the roof of his car, the metronomic 'thump, thump, thump' of windscreen wipers lulling him to sleep. He awoke abruptly to the realisation that his car was no longer cruising along the smooth surface of the road but rather, it was hurtling down an embankment. Startled, he grabbed the steering wheel and tried to regain control of the vehicle. Suddenly, a light post came into view. 'Don't hit it!' He thought to himself in a panic. But it seemed to jump out at him, crumpling the bonnet of his car, glass shattering onto his lap as he jerked to a halt. Dazed, he sat amongst the shattered glass and debris until an ambulance arrived. As he was lifted onto the stretcher, an ambulance officer spoke to him gently, doing her best to ensure he didn't lose consciousness.

"I don't understand," Josh murmured.

"What don't you understand?" She asked.

"The car was heading towards an empty field. There was nothing around… except that lamp post. I kept thinking 'don't hit it, don't hit it…' so why? Why out of all that empty space, did I hit the one object in the field?"

"Ah," she replied, knowingly. "Happens all the time. Didn't you know? What you focus on, is what you hit."

What are you focussing on?

If you're focussing on your fears, unwittingly, you might be hurtling straight towards them.

*'Don't fret or worry. Instead of worrying, pray. Let petitions and **praises** shape your worries into prayers, letting God know your concerns. Before you know it, a sense of God's wholeness, everything coming together for good, will come and settle you down. It's wonderful what happens when Christ displaces worry at the center of your life.'* Philippians 4:7 (emphasis mine)

The 'petition' part is easy – when you're afraid, getting on your knees and pleading with God for help is a natural reaction. But what's with this 'praise' business? Is there anything you feel like doing *less* than issuing praises when you're focussed on the terror that lies before you?

Perhaps that's the point. Praise redirects your attention from the thing you fear most, to the one who can save you from it. Thanking God through praise, helps you to remember everything He's done for you. I know it hurts. That's why in Hebrews 13:15 it's called a 'Sacrifice of Praise.' But recalling those times He's come through for you when you needed Him most will be an incredible source of peace and comfort.

Take your eyes off Him and the battle may appear lost... but SPOILER ALERT: God's got this.

As always, everything God asks of us is for our good. Reminding us to praise Him in the storm isn't the demand of a dictator, but rather the prescription of a healer.

Read Matthew 14:22-33 – It's one of my favourite bible stories. Jesus' disciples are far out at sea in a boat, battered by the waves, when they see Jesus walking towards them on the water. Wait. What? I can't imagine how I'd respond if I saw someone walking on water under *any* circumstances, let alone amongst battering waves.

Naturally, they're all terrified at first, but Peter remembers that this is Jesus, after all, so in an incredible act of faith, or recklessness (or both) he jumps out of the boat...

Jumping out of the boat, Peter walked on the water to Jesus. But when he looked down at the waves churning beneath his feet, he lost his nerve and started to sink. He cried, "Master, save me!" Matthew 14:30

See what happened there? While Peter's focus was on Jesus, remembering who Jesus is and what he's capable of, Peter was capable of the supernatural (eg walking on water) but as soon as his focus shifted to what was going on around him, he started to sink.

Sound familiar? Not the walking on water part, but the focussing on what scares you most, rather than the one who can reach down and pull you out of it, if only you'll let him.

Jesus didn't hesitate. He reached down and grabbed his hand. Then he said, "Faint-heart, what got into you?" Matthew 14:31

I love that Jesus never loses patience with our lack of faith and focus. His response is so gentle and kind. A stark contrast to how I sometimes react when my little ones are disobedient! And that line 'He reached down and grabbed his hand.' What a beautiful metaphor for salvation. Jesus reached down and grabbed your hand when you fell beneath the waves of life. You needed only to cry out as Peter did *"Master, save me!"*

For so many of us, the fear that grips us, especially as parents, comes when we shift our focus from Jesus and onto the evening news. Do that and it's not too long before fear grips your heart. The world can seem a very dark place.

NBC's Fred Rogers famously said: "When I was a boy and I would see scary things in the news, my mother would say to me, 'Look for the helpers. You will always find people who are helping.'"

On April 15, 2013, two pressure cooker bombs exploded during the Boston Marathon, killing three and wounding about 264 others.

I watched the footage in horror and disbelief but something that struck me amongst the chaos that followed the explosion was that amongst the sea of people running away, a few ran against the tide, in the direction of the blasts. Every instinct inside my body would demand that I run away, what was it that compelled these people to run towards danger? These were the helpers Fred's mother was talking about. These are the people who God gifts to us in our darkest moments.

When my eldest was six months old, I was in a state of sleep deprived delirium one morning when I took something downstairs to the bin. As I lifted the lid, it suddenly occurred to me that it was bin day and the clunking engine sounds of the garbage truck lurching toward our street filled my ears.

In a panic, I pushed the bin down our steep driveway, careful not to be dragged down with it and there I stood, in slippers and track pants, resplendent with wild hair and vomit encrusted shirt. That's when I heard it. At first, I thought I'd imagined it but then I heard it again. Unmistakable now. The terrified screams of a woman coming from somewhere in our street. This woman was clearly in danger and frightened for her life.

I glanced up our driveway, thinking to myself 'why, oh why, didn't I get my hubby to bring the bin down? He'd know what to do!' I realised that apart from the sounds of a garbage truck in the distance, there was no one else around to answer the cries of this poor woman.

So, I took a few, trembling steps forward, drawn by her horrific screams. Pictures of mafia gangs, a dank basement and zip ties filling my mind. What on earth was I getting into?

As I walked carefully down the street, trying to find the source of the screams, I soon realised they were emanating from the house two doors down. The house which had been on the market for months and, as far as I knew, was empty.

Knees knocking, I slowly climbed the stairs, the unbearable screaming now loud and clear.

"H-h-h-h-hello?' I said. Almost a whisper. Almost hoping no one would respond.

The screaming intensified. Growing ever more frantic and incoherent.

"Should I call the police?" I called gingerly, imagining a giant 'baddy' about to lunge through the door at any moment. I realised belatedly that my phone was back at home, where I wished very much that I was, too.

"NO! Police can't help me!" She screamed back.

"An ambulance?"

"NO!" She replied, followed by more incoherent babble.

"I'm so sorry," I responded. "I can't understand a word you're saying. Can you please slow down and tell me what's happened?"

A deep sigh. "Okay," she said, almost calm now. "I'm trapped in the toilet and I'm running out of air. My daughter's gone out and won't be back until tonight. The doors are all locked so you can't get in to let me out."

"Okay, what's your daughter's phone number?"

"I don't know."

"Where has she gone?" I asked.

"I don't know." She cried. Then she paused. "She's gone to a doctor's surgery. Somewhere near a 7 eleven."

"I think I know the one," I replied. "How about if I drive down there and ask her to let you out."

"Oh, thank you. Thank you. Thank you so much." She sobbed in gratitude and relief. Her salvation was at hand!

"Alright, I'll go and do that. You just sit tight." And with that, My slippered feet lunged down the stairs and I ran breathlessly home, relieved that no goons were chasing me.

"I'm off to the doctor's," I yelled over my shoulder at my befuddled husband. "I'll tell you when I get home."

I walked into the medical centre, put my elbows on the reception desk and said, "This is the strangest conversation you're going to have today." Her eyes met mine and I knew I had her full attention.

"I believe there's a lady in this surgery whose mother is trapped in a toilet. She needs to come home and let her out."

I told her the name of the person I was looking for and without saying a word, she pointed to the back of the waiting room.

There she was, filling out a new patient form, completely unaware of the circumstances that would lead her to meet her new neighbour in such an unorthodox fashion.

"Hi," I said, trying to be as unwierd as possible. She looked up from her form, curious.

"I'm your new neighbour and this is the strangest conversation you're going to have today." I had her full attention. "Your mother is trapped in the toilet and she needs you to let her out."

"Right," she said, putting the new patient form in her lap and pondering her next move.

"I'll go back and let her know you're on your way?"

"That would be wonderful," she said, still computing what she'd just been told.

I drove back and, still in my slippers, climbed the stairs of the house two doors down for the second time that day.

"Hello?" I said.

"Hello!" Came the response, full of expectation.

"Your daughter is on her way." I could almost feel the weight lifting from her shoulders.

"Thank you!" She cried.

The sound of a car pulling up in the street below announced her daughter's arrival. Freedom was imminent.

I bet the air never smelt sweeter as she took her first breaths outside that oxygen deprived toilet.

That afternoon, I sat on the deck with my little one, pondering the events of the morning, when I heard a familiar shout coming from the street below.

"Hello!" I recognised the voice, but not the face. "I'm the old lady you rescued from the toilet this morning." She was holding a giant bunch of flowers. "You saved my life," she said, the gratitude clear in her eyes.

Isaiah 52:7 says, *'How beautiful on the mountains are the feet of the messenger bringing good news, Breaking the news that all's well, proclaiming good times, announcing salvation.'*

How beautiful on the steps of her house my slippered feet must have sounded that morning. I'm sure Peter felt similarly grateful as he took his first gulps of air after being pulled from the depths of the ocean by the gentle hand of Jesus. All the greater my gratitude at finding myself pulled from the depths of my own sin.

One of my favourite quotes from J. R. R. Tolkien's The [8]Two Towers is an exchange between Sam and Frodo:

"It's like in the great stories, Mr. Frodo. The ones that really mattered. Full of darkness and danger they were. And sometimes you didn't want to know the end. Because how could the end be happy? How could the world go back to the way it was when so

much bad had happened? But in the end, it's only a passing thing, this shadow. Even darkness must pass. A new day will come. And when the sun shines it will shine out the clearer. Those were the stories that stayed with you. That meant something, even if you were too small to understand why. But I think, Mr. Frodo, I do understand. I know now. Folk in those stories had lots of chances of turning back, only they didn't. They kept going, because they were holding on to something. That there is some good in this world, and it's worth fighting for."

And a word of comfort from Paul: *'I'm absolutely convinced that nothing—nothing living or dead, angelic or demonic, today or tomorrow, high or low, thinkable or unthinkable—absolutely nothing can get between us and God's love because of the way that Jesus our Master has embraced us.' Romans 8:38-39*

Now *that's* something to be grateful for!

And sometimes, in the midst of fear, you just need to keep quiet and let God work. I've already discussed, in chapter 2, how God inhabits the praises of His people. But what about negative talk?

"If you don't have anything nice to say, don't say anything at all." I'm sure that, like me, you grew up rolling your eyes whenever this little pearl of wisdom was quoted at you, usually because I'd just said something particularly unkind. But what if negative talk has spiritual implications? Suddenly it's not just about good manners, but a matter of spiritual victory that's at stake.

When the Israelites stood on the shores of the Red Sea, grumbling and complaining as the Egyptians were fast approaching, Moses says, *"God will fight the battle for you. And you? You keep your mouths shut!"* Exodus 14:14

And as they prepared to march around Jericho, Joshua's instruction was, *"Don't shout. In fact, don't even speak—not so much as a whisper…"* Joshua 6:10

I'm sure there were a few reasons for this, not least of all the fact that by day 3 or 4, the Israelites would likely have started mumbling things like "My feet hurt, my back's killing me and let me tell you about my chafing situation." Joshua didn't need those negative vibes getting in the way of what God had planned.

Even Jesus would not allow negative talk to get in the way of a miracle. When he enters the home of a girl who's been declared dead, the first thing he does is to tell everyone who's spreading negativity to leave the room.

"He permitted no one to go in with him except Peter, James, and John. They entered the leader's house and pushed their way through the gossips looking for a story and neighbours bringing in casseroles. Jesus was abrupt: "Why all this busybody grief and gossip? This child isn't dead; she's sleeping." Provoked to sarcasm, they told him he didn't know what he was talking about. But when he had sent them all out, he took the child's father and mother, along with his companions, and entered the child's room. He clasped the girl's hand and said, "Talitha koum," which means, "Little girl, get up." At that, she was up and walking around! This girl was twelve years of age. They, of course, were all beside themselves with joy. He gave them strict orders that no one was to know what had taken place in that room. Then he said, "Give her something to eat." Mark 5:37-43

I love that Jesus is interested in both the miraculous and the practical, bringing the girl back to life and knowing that she must be hungry following her deathly experience.

The same was true for Elijah in 1 Kings 19, when he fled for his life upon hearing about Jezebel's plot to kill him. Alone, exhausted and terrified, he falls asleep under a bush and then an angel wakes him up to give him bread and water. He sleeps again and is awoken by the same angel to eat and drink.

Then, over a 40 day journey, he makes his way to the mountain of God and when God asks what he's doing there, he answers in frantic, babbling, fearful sentences, much like my poor neighbour when I first asked her what was wrong. In response, God tells him to stand on top of the mountain as He passes by.

1 Kings 19:12-14 says *A hurricane wind ripped through the mountains and shattered the rocks before God, but God wasn't to be found in the wind; after the wind an earthquake, but God wasn't in the earthquake; and after the earthquake fire, but God wasn't in the fire; and after the fire a gentle and quiet whisper. When Elijah heard the quiet voice, he muffled his face with his great cloak, went to the mouth of the cave, and stood there. A quiet voice asked, "So Elijah, now tell me, what are you doing here?"*

Yes, God is the God of the wind, the earthquake and the fire. But sometimes we need to hear from the God of the gentle, quiet whisper to reassure us that He is still Master of it all.

Practice Makes Perfect

'KEEP YOUR EYES OPEN FOR GOD, *watch for his works;*
BE ALERT FOR SIGNS OF *his presence.*
REMEMBER THE WORLD OF WONDERS *he has made.*' Psalm 105:4-5

"Spotto!" If you've ever been on a road trip with kids, you'll know all about this game. The idea is to be the first to call out "spotto" when you spot a yellow car on the road. The person who's the first to call out "spotto" the most on any given trip, wins bragging rights for about 10 minutes after arriving at your destination.

You may not be aware of a lesser known addition to the game: "Snotto." This requires calling out "snotto" at the top of your lungs when you see a green car. The inspiration for this name is both obvious and hilarious to any child under the age of 10.

I must admit that the first time my kids introduced me to this game on our daily drive to school, I was sceptical. I mean, hardly anyone owns a yellow car, or even less likely, a green one, right? I was prepared for two very bored and disappointed little boys. Well, I was soon to be proven wrong. Who knew there were so many yellow and green cars zooming around our neighbourhood? Barely a minute went by before we were all yelling gleefully at the top of our lungs "spotto!" These yellow and green cars had always been there, and now I had just adjusted my vision so I could *see* them.

Any parent will tell you that we're not born grateful. Entitlement runs thick in our veins from birth. Don't expect a 'thank you' from your newborn after her 3am feed and nappy change but she'll certainly let you know when she's ready to do it all again! It's a natural survival instinct to make noise until we get what we want. Finding contentment is what's supernatural.

So how do we cultivate gratitude? The simple answer is; with practice.

After the birth of my first child, I was surprised to find myself struggling with Post-Natal Depression. Our baby was very much wanted (I had struggled with infertility for 3 years) and I was beyond elated when he was born. But an unexpected side effect of motherhood is the seeming loss of identity that comes with it. I had been a successful career woman, with a business card that told everyone (including myself) exactly who I was. But there's no business card for motherhood and it hit me just how much I had found my identity in what I did for a living, rather than who I really was within.

It's usually the first question asked at dinner parties; "So, what do you do for a living?" The answer seems to tell us everything we need to know, or assume, about someone.

My loss of identity left me in somewhat of a rut, until someone suggested I start a Gratitude Journal. I was willing to try anything to lift myself out of my depressed state.

My assignment was simple: Write down 5 things you're thankful for each day. So, on Day 1 I sat on my bed, pen in hand and stared at the blank page. 'What do I have to be thankful for today?' I pondered. I really struggled to come up with 5 things for my list, but I persevered. For the first week or so, it was hard work, but the more I practiced being grateful, the easier it became.

I found myself making mental notes throughout the day. For instance, someone would give up their seat for me on the bus and I'd think 'well, that's going in my Gratitude Journal.' I became very deliberate at looking for things to be thankful for and making a mental note of them, until it became an integral part of my day. Soon, noticing these things was as natural as breathing to me.

My morning walks became my prayer walk. Watching the sun rise and the birds welcoming the day with their morning symphony, it's almost impossible not to feel grateful. I've even been known to raise my hands in the air and bask in God's goodness as I meander along the footpath. What a great way to start the day!

Over time, my mood lifted and finally happiness became my default emotion again, rather than depression.

These things I had to be thankful for had always been there, I had just adjusted my thinking to see them.

'You're blessed when you get your inside world—your mind and heart—put right. Then you can see God in the outside world.'
Matthew 5:8

Take time to literally stop and smell the roses and lift up a prayer of thanks as you do. Smile to yourself when you're blessed with a great car park, when an old friend calls, when you lie in fresh sheets, when the sun warms your face on a cold day, when your child sits in your lap for a cuddle. Don't let these moments hurtle by unnoticed. Note them down, then on the days when you're feeling blue, read through your Gratitude Journal and remind yourself of all the things you have to be thankful for, and don't forget the thank the Gift Giver.

I have started a running list of all the things that make me smile. Here are my first 25 entries, that might help inspire you to start your own.

1. Morning cuddles in bed – especially when it's cold outside.
2. Trying new flavours… and liking them!
3. Slippers and tracksuit pants at the end of a long day.
4. Birds. Their song. Their presence.
5. My son's 'tight squeeze' hugs around my neck.
6. Rain… when we don't need to go anywhere.
7. A late night, spontaneous visit from a friend.
8. Clear blue, cloudless skies.
9. An orange and purple sunset.
10. Giggly whispers with my boys.
11. When my youngest says 'you're my best.'
12. Peace + quiet + coffee.
13. A leafy view.
14. Saturday mornings with no alarm.

15. When my boys kick a goal.
16. When someone says they're praying for me.
17. Fresh sheets.
18. Quiet time on the deck.
19. Hubby at home making pizza.
20. Mist covered fields on early morning walks.
21. Someone has a prophetic word for me.
22. Receiving a birthday party invitation.
23. The sound of my children laughing.
24. Hearing my new favourite song for the first time.
25. Losing myself in a good book.

Reading through this list makes me smile every time.

Here are some ideas to help encourage a culture of gratitude in your home and in your life…

- Each night at the dinner table, ask everyone what they're grateful for about the day.
- Get everyone to start a Gratitude Journal and document 5 things they're grateful for each day. On a tough day, it's a great way to remember how blessed you are.
- Keep reminding those around you of all the things you're grateful for about them and encourage them to talk about the things they're grateful for about each other.
- Wherever possible, remember to look for the silver lining in every situation.

'Every desirable and beneficial gift comes out of heaven. The gifts are rivers of light cascading down from the Father of Light.' James 1:17-18

A while ago, one of my friends felt God was showing her white feathers as a reminder that He was thinking of her. This was something very personal between her and God. They just kept showing up in unexpected places and to her it was as if God was buying her a bunch of flowers every day.

I remember standing at my kitchen sink one afternoon and I said to God 'You know what, I'd love to have a white feather, too. Just as a little special moment between You and me.' I didn't ask out of jealousy. Not even a little bit. I just thought it was really nice and something I would love to experience, too.

You know what? I looked down into my kitchen sink and guess what was just sitting there…? Yup… a big old white feather! There was absolutely no reason for a feather of *any* description to be sitting, untouched, in my sink. It's not even near a window! It was just a little moment between me and God and I'll never forget it.

Some months later, I was feeling depleted, overwhelmed with life and wondering if God's favour was still upon me. I remember sitting in traffic one morning, tears streaming down my cheeks and I cried out to God: 'If I'm still in your favour, please show me. Give me the comfort of Your presence.' In that moment, a white feather floated down from the sky. It kissed the front tip of my bonnet, then glided up, over my windscreen, down over my rear vision mirror and then drifted effortlessly to the very rear tip of my boot and then disappeared. I laughed out loud. Thank God for the gift of awareness! My heart was filled with warmth and assurance that yes, I was still resting in His favour and oh, how He loves me.

Ask God to open your eyes to the little gifts He's been placing in front of you all along.

The God Who Sees Me

BUSINESS OWNERSHIP IS LIKE RIDING a rollercoaster that never stops. As you reach a peak, and you're full of exhilaration, an inevitable descent soon follows. Sometimes you're upside down, sometimes back-to-front, often on top, but never still.

There was one particular point on my ride that nearly broke me. We had engaged a new contractor to work on a project that was beyond our scope at the time. We paid him thousands of dollars on behalf of our client to do the work up front (yes, I know, rookie mistake). Soon after, his phone number stopped working and his emails bounced back. He had skipped town with our money and I was left holding the proverbial baby. It was devastating.

I was absolutely determined not to let our client down, so I decided to take on the project myself. What followed was months of struggle and pain. I physically felt the weight of what I was carrying. My neck and shoulders ached with the strain and eventually I descended into depression. I cried out to God for breakthrough, but His silence was deafening.

I remember driving into the city every day, worship music blaring and singing at the top of my lungs - declaring victory, breakthrough and every other promise I could think of. I didn't care if I looked crazy to the commuters around me, this was between me and God.

But breakthrough didn't come, and the burden got heavier and heavier. I was choking on the pressure. One night I dreamt that I was in prison. It was dark and dingy; the food was terrible and the company wasn't any better. I woke up in the morning and told my husband about my dream. I said "that prison felt like a holiday compared to what I'm living through right now." That's how dire it felt.

It all came to a head the day before Good Friday. I thought my breakthrough had come and the project was working perfectly. But it literally crashed before my eyes and I burst into tears. These were angry tears. Tears of frustration and abandonment. One thing was for sure; I did NOT feel like going to church on Good Friday and facing God. I was so mad at Him.

Well, the next morning I dragged myself out of bed and as we pulled into the church car park, it took every ounce of my will power to get out of the car. I was furious with God.

I sat in the pew, shoulders hunched, praying no one came over to talk to me. The worship band kicked off, we all got to our feet and I stood in silence. I couldn't even bring myself to sing. I was having it out with God in my head. 'How could you do this to me? Where are you? Why are you ignoring me? Well, I don't feel like talking to you, either!'

I don't remember a word of the sermon, I just sat there brooding and waiting to get back into the car so I could cry in peace at home.

I'm really embarrassed now looking back at my 'petulant child' impression.

As the service ended, my husband touched my arm and said "I'll get the kids and meet you in the car." He knew I wasn't up for hanging around!

But as I stood up, one of the men in the church who has a prophetic gift ran over to me, bursting with excitement. He said, "I've got a word for you!" My husband stood beside me, with his arm around me while this dear man spoke God's heart over me. He said, "As I was watching you during the worship service..." (the same worship service I spent yelling at God in my mind) "I could see creativity just pouring out of you. You have an incredible creative gift and it just radiates from you. I saw a chef in a bakery and there was a cake in front of him. He was putting icing into the piping bag and he started squeezing the bag. Right there, where the squeezing is taking place... that's you right now. You're being squeezed beyond what you think you can handle and you feel like you're about to explode, but what is going to come out, is something so beautiful. He's using the icing in that piping bag to decorate that cake and a beautiful creation is being formed. Does that mean anything to you?"

I burst into tears. But not angry tears this time. They were tears of elation. 'God *sees* me!' This man had no idea what I had been going through, or even that I have a creative gift. He was purely speaking God's words over me and I could finally see God's hand over this whole situation. He hadn't abandoned me at all. He was there with me in the darkness, and more importantly, He *sees* me.

I remember sitting in my garden that afternoon, feeling completely at peace. My, how my perspective changed with just this simple revelation: God sees me.

Come Easter Sunday morning, I bounced out of bed. I couldn't wait to sing His praises again.

Eventually, an expert offered to help with the project and we were able to follow it through to completion. What a relief!

A few months later, I went on a morning walk with my youngest. We meandered along the riverbank and paused to skim stones along the crystal-clear waters. It's such a beautiful memory. When we got home, I jumped in the shower and to my horror, I found a lump in my breast. I froze with fear. This is a moment every woman dreads. I was able to get an appointment with my GP that morning and was scheduled for a mammogram a few days later. I remember standing in my kitchen and I wanted to scream out loud. I realised that months of carrying this heavy burden that was never mine to carry, had taken its toll on my body. The stress, sleepless nights and perpetually clenched fists were toxic to my health.

Waiting for the diagnosis was a surreal time. I was so mindful of everything around me. Would I get to see my kids grow up? How many Christmases and birthdays do I have left? I will never say 'no' when my child asks me to read to him or give him a cuddle. How many more cuddles will I get to experience?

A few days later, my GP called me in to discuss the results and Praise God, the lump was benign. I burst into tears of relief and she asked if I was okay. I said, 'I've spent the last year in a place of death and now I just want to live!'

Fast forward a couple of years and our business hit another giant hurdle – The COVID-19 pandemic. Our state was put into 'lockdown' and many businesses were forced to close their doors. It wasn't long before a major client called to say they were closing and the financial hit to our business was significant but Phil and I both looked at each other and smiled. What I had learnt two years before had changed my life. I knew that 'God's got this.' We both felt completely at peace during that season and recognised it as an 'incubation period.' I saw the lockdown as my chrysalis and the quiet time in our business as an opportunity to invest time in some 'heart projects' that I hadn't been able to work on during the busyness of business life (including writing this book!). As always, God brought us through to the other side of that season, and I didn't try to carry the burden on my own. That made all the difference.

Of course, I'm not the first to feel abandoned by God and as if I were carrying the weight of the world on my shoulders. David said it better than I ever could:

'Long enough, God—
you've ignored me long enough.
I've looked at the back of your head
long enough. Long enough
I've carried this ton of trouble,
lived with a stomach full of pain.' Psalm 13:1-2

But then in the very next Psalm he says: *'God is around; God turns life around.'* Psalm 14:7

Then there's Hagar; impregnated by her boss's husband (Abram) then bullied to the point of running away.

She finds herself sitting beside a spring, feeling utterly abandoned, when an angel shows up and tells her everything will be okay.

'She answered God by name, praying to the God who spoke to her, "You're the God who sees me!" Yes! He saw me; and then I saw him!" That's how that desert spring got named "God-Alive-Sees-Me Spring."' Genesis 16:13-14

A few centuries later, another woman stood alone at a well but this time it was Jesus, rather than an angel, who spoke to her. In John 4:7-30, after her encounter with Jesus, she returns to her village declaring; *"Come see a man who knew all about the things I did, who knows me inside and out."*

This is truly a life-changing revelation: God sees you. Whatever you're going through right now. Whatever burden you're carrying. God sees you.

I asked my friends to share their stories about when they've felt 'seen' by God…

When my Dad was dying and in Palliative Care, I was not saved, but I still prayed. On my Dad's final day on earth I remember praying; 'God if you are there, then I'm letting you know that I'm selfish and I cannot bear to watch my Dad suffer any longer, please I beg you to take him home.' Dad died 3 hours later. This started my 12 month journey to salvation. His death made me realise that true healing comes in death. Then one night while camping, I woke to what I thought was my daughter's voice. I nudged my husband to go check her as it was his turn ('Mother of the Year' moment). He screamed for me, and I came racing over. My daughter was foaming at the mouth, her lips going blue, her whole body shaking uncontrollably. I told my husband to "Call an ambulance! She's having a massive seizure!" He went outside to call.

I was praying in tongues over her and in that moment my heart realised that even though I was a highly trained, highly qualified health professional, I could do nothing to save my child. The seizure had been going for over 3 minutes. I prayed these words to God: "I can't save her Lord, but you can, I give her back to you, whatever happens I trust you, your will be done." The moment I finished the prayer, her seizure stopped. Two miracles: 1. During a seizure it is almost unheard of to speak, so I do believe the Holy Spirit used my daughter's voice to wake me so I could go to her. 2. The seizure only stopped when I gave God back what was His.

I spent the last week of my Mum's life staying with her day and night in Palliative Care. I heard her stir three nights before she died. I got up and went to her and she held my arm. I lay beside her. She said, "Why do you think God hasn't taken me home yet?" I said, "I don't know, but if you are here, then you still have purpose." She said, "Can you sing to me 'Victory we have in Jesus'?" I only knew those 5 words. We laughed and I lay with her a while longer. These parts of my life have been painful, but even when God is silent, He is working in us and through us. He sees us and knows when to speak and when to wait for us to surrender our agenda, to look up and seek Him; The only one who can truly carry us through. – Kirra

My husband was finishing off a degree through a training provider called QANTUM and we were so broke, with three kids to feed. I was worried, it was weighing me down and filling my mind so that I felt like I couldn't hear from God. As I was walking through the supermarket one day, carrying this anxiety around with me and feeling so far from God, I said "God, I just really need writing on the wall. No more mystery. I can't hear your voice right now, so I need you to show me what to do." I turned the corner and right there in front of me was a giant advertisement for a dishwashing product and it said 'FINISH QANTUM.' I would never normally have noticed an ad like that because we don't have a dishwasher but there it was, the writing on the wall, and I instantly felt peace. - Jesse

I was chatting with my neighbour and she asked me to share with her why I'd become a Christian, so I was telling her about God's goodness and love in my life. Later, she reminded me that it was her wedding anniversary that day. I felt terrible because I'd really wanted to bless her and her husband with a gift and had completely forgotten all about it! It was time to get dinner ready and bathe the kids so I couldn't duck out and buy something. I asked the Lord for help. Then there was a knock on the door and one of our church pastors was standing there with a big gift basket in his hands. I'd been nominated by someone at our church to receive a gift basket! I was so excited to receive this wonderful gift but then I had a sudden realisation; 'God has answered my prayer! This gift basket isn't for me, it's for my neighbour!' Once my kids got over the disappointment that the gift basket was for someone else, they made a beautiful card for our neighbours and were so excited to take the gift basket to them. I was able to share with neighbours the story of God's provision and it blessed all of us. – Kara

I'd been going through a really rough time with one of my kids. I was losing sleep, and feeling anxious all the time. I went for a walk one day to clear my head and listened to a podcast. The speaker started declaring passionately "We've been surrounded and battered by troubles, but we're not demoralized; we're not sure what to do, but we know that God knows what to do; we've been spiritually terrorized, but God hasn't left our side; we've been thrown down, but we haven't broken." (2 Corinthians 4:8). I felt that message was directed straight at me. Fast forward a few months and things had gotten worse with my teen. I was so disheartened and anxious. I put on my headphones again and started listening to a different podcast. This speaker passionately declared the same verse! I knew it was God's way of saying that He was with me during this long, dark season. Some storms go for a really long time but I know God is still working and He still sees me. – Ricayla

One day I told my 7 year old son your story about the white feather in your sink and how it reminded you that God sees you. He said, "I want a feather too, mummy!" While I was busy wrapping up something inside, he set out on a bit of a 'treasure hunt' around the yard but there was no sign of a white feather. He came to me disappointed and I explained that we don't need to search for it, God will just show us and maybe God has a different way to show him. I sat with him on a hill in our backyard and we prayed. As soon as we finished, he noticed on the grass a beautiful white feather and was overjoyed. He picked it up and with a great big grin on his face he said, "God sees me, mum!" As we walked a hundred metres back into our house white feathers were everywhere - he must have found 10 more feathers right on the path we had just walked down only minutes prior. We reflected that this shows that we don't need to search for God's promises and goodness - we just need to ask. Afterwards, he prayed and asked God to let him know if that would be his sign forever that Jesus is with him. That night, Jesus appeared to him in a dream. In the morning he said, "Mum the feathers are definitely Jesus saying 'I'm here' but even if I never see feathers it's okay, because Jesus told me he's there anyway." He sees white feathers all the time now and he's reminded each time that Jesus is with him, whether he sees a feather or not. – Renee

SEEING GOD

When I was about twenty years old, I'd been in church on a Sunday morning and left to have coffee in the church hall with friends. Sometime later, about to head home, I realised that I'd left my Bible in the chapel, so went back for it. The chapel was deserted, except for two older ladies standing and chatting in the doorway. I knew them, so I stopped to ask how they were. I also asked one of them, Mrs Nel, how her daughter was, as I was a friend of hers but we'd both started studies in different places and hadn't been in touch for a while. Mrs Nel said that she and her friend had just been praying about her daughter in the chapel, that they would receive some sort of word to confirm or deny their fears for her. She had been taking a gap year and working on a farm for mentally disabled folk. They lived in family groups, were cared for, and did some subsistence farming. Mrs Nel and her friend were worried that it may be a bit of a religious cult. I couldn't believe God's timing! A few months before, as part of my teaching experience, some friends and I had been placed on that exact farm to do work experience. None of us Christian students had had any peace within our spirits there, and discovered that there was indeed a cult at work. It was no coincidence that I had stumbled upon these ladies and was able to share my story, and we all marvelled at how God had orchestrated us to meet. God is always in control and they were able to have insight into my friend's situation. I'm in awe of the way God moves and that at times he chooses to use us in His plans! - Pam

Supernatural Satisfaction

—

'YOU'RE BLESSED WHEN YOU'RE CONTENT *with just who you are – no more, no less. That's the moment you find yourselves proud owners of everything that can't be bought.'* Matthew 5:5

It was beginning to look a lot like Christmas and our Sunday School Choir was busy rehearsing for our big Christmas show.

A cacophony of exuberant (if not angelic) voices filled the church hall. We were all singing our little hearts out, and I was front and centre. Mainly because I was the shortest 8-year-old in the group, rather than any vocal talent. I could not have been more excited about my centre-stage debut.

Our mothers had busied themselves transforming white sheets into angelic robes and we each donned a halo made from tinsel. I felt thoroughly divine as I made my way to the front row at dress rehearsal. Then suddenly, out of the corner of my eye, something sparkly grabbed my attention. Karen in the third row was not dressed like the rest of us. Her mother was a professional seamstress and she had whipped up the sparkliest, most extravagantly angelic costume ever to grace the stage, resplendent with 'beauty queen' style tiara in place of the standard tinsel halo.

Envy boiled up inside me and I turned to face her, hands on hips. My angel costume, which had moments before brought me so much joy, was now the ugliest, most awful fashion disaster I'd ever been subjected to wearing.

Let's just say, the incident ended with me being dragged off stage, and the dress rehearsal going ahead without me, while I received a thorough 'attitude adjustment' from my mother, backstage.

Fast forward a few decades and I was a slightly delirious, sleep deprived new mother. That's the reason, I tell myself, why I felt like punching my computer screen when I read a post from a friend, who also had a newborn, boasting that her little cherub was already sleeping through the night.

Parenting can feel like a competitive sport sometimes… "My boy just toilet trained himself. How's yours doing with the bed wetting?" Or "I gave birth drug free. Tell me all about your epidural."

Encounters like this can easily take the shine off a simultaneously tumultuous and glorious season of life. I had to consciously stop comparing myself to other parents and my kids to theirs because it was stealing my joy.

Enjoying each moment, as though it could be you last, rather than focussing on unhealthy comparisons, is the secret to true contentment.

If today *was* your last day on earth, how would you spend it? I asked several friends and these are some of their responses...

Eat my favourite foods all day.

Spend it with my family.

Tell my loved ones how I really feel about them and leave nothing unsaid.

Visit all my favourite places one last time.

Cuddle my pets.

It's not surprising that all responses were centred around ourselves (including my own response) and ensuring our last day on earth was a positive one.

What strikes me as so incredible about Jesus is that when he knew it was his last day on earth (before his death and resurrection), he washed feet, he gave thanks, and prayed... alone.

While he was on earth, Jesus didn't pursue equality with anyone, including God. He lived humbly and selflessly, in obedience to the point of death (Philippians 2:7-8) and he came to be known as the Servant King.

Even as he was dying an excruciating and humiliating death on the cross, he made sure his mother would be taken care of and asked God to forgive everyone involved in his death.

Also, Jesus was satisfied with so little.

When someone asked if he could follow Jesus, his response was priceless; *"Are you ready to rough it? We're not staying in the best inns, you know."* (Luke 9:57-58)

What a stark contrast to the events that took place in the Garden of Eden. Adam and Eve were completely satisfied - until someone told them there was more, and they were missing out.

Was the 'original sin' just an act of disobedience, or was it something far deeper than that?

Does any of this sound familiar…? You love your house, but you can't help noticing that your neighbour's deck has a nicer outlook than yours. You're happy with your big screen TV, but your friend has a slightly bigger one and wow, their picture quality is incredible. And you love your kids… but wouldn't it be nice if they were high achievers like your brother's kids?

'Don't love the world's ways. Don't love the world's goods. Love of the world squeezes out love for the Father. Practically everything that goes on in the world—wanting your own way, wanting everything for yourself, wanting to appear important—has nothing to do with the Father. It just isolates you from him. The world and all its wanting, wanting, wanting is on the way out—but whoever does what God wants is set for eternity.' 1 John 2:15

In Genesis 4, the serpent tells Eve, *"God knows that the moment you eat from that tree, you'll see what's really going on."* The desire for importance and equality with God was all it took to convince Eve to eat the one thing she was told not to. It was a matter of the heart and not just an action that separated Adam and Eve from God.

'If God gives such attention to the appearance of wildflowers—most of which are never even seen—don't you think he'll attend to you, take pride in you, do his best for you? What I'm trying to do here is to get you to relax, to not be so preoccupied with getting, so

you can respond to God's giving. People who don't know God and the way he works fuss over these things, but you know both God and how he works. Steep your life in God-reality, God-initiative, God-provisions. Don't worry about missing out. You'll find all your everyday human concerns will be met.' Matthew 6:33

This sentiment is reiterated in Luke 12:29-32: *'What I'm trying to do here is get you to relax, not be so preoccupied with getting so you can respond to God's giving. People who don't know God and the way he works fuss over these things, but you know both God and how he works. Steep yourself in God-reality, God-initiative, God-provisions. You'll find all your everyday human concerns will be met. Don't be afraid of missing out. You're my dearest friends! The Father wants to give you the very kingdom itself.'*

Did you know that humans do not have a reference point for satisfaction? We humans experience satisfaction in direct relation to what's happening around us.

This explains the dramatic increase in depression since the advent of Social Media. You can spend hours scrolling through the 'highlight reels' of your friends' lives online. But how many of your friends are sharing their outtakes and failures? Your own happiness can be easily diminished when you believe others around you have more.

Don't believe me?

A [9]study conducted at the University of Miami found that people would prefer to earn a lower income, as long as their co-workers earnt even less, rather than to earn more while their co-workers earnt more than they did.

If you ask any wealthy person, "How much money is enough?" most will respond with, "Just a little bit more."

But of course, the bible told us about that centuries ago, *'The one who loves money is never satisfied with money, Nor the one who loves wealth with big profits. More smoke.'* Ecclesiastes 5:10

Supernatural satisfaction comes from understanding that we are children of the God who says, *"All creation and its bounty are mine."* Psalm 50:10-15

When God is our reference point for satisfaction, we should *never* experience jealousy. I know my God has everything I need and when I align my thoughts with His thoughts, I'm always satisfied.

Psalm 37:4 in the NIV says, *'Take delight in the Lord, and he will give you the desires of your heart.'*

What it took me a while to realise is that when I delight myself in Him, He *is* the desire of my heart. When my friend gets a promotion, or a party invitation, or their kid gets an award, I'm genuinely happy for them and cheering them on. Because my delight isn't in achievements or acquiring things, my delight and my identity is in the deeper things of God. Everything else is a bonus.

My God owns all of creation *and 'Every desirable and beneficial gift comes out of heaven. The gifts are rivers of light cascading down from the Father of Light. There is nothing deceitful in God, nothing two-faced, nothing fickle. He brought us to life using the true Word, showing us off as the crown of all his creatures.'* James 1:17

Sometimes, it can be tempting to feel as though you need to earn a salvation so grand, and this, in itself, can lead to a life of perpetual exhaustion and comparison.

When I was a new Christian, I was so afraid of turning back to my old ways, that I filled every spare minute of my time serving in the church. I attended two bible study groups a week, volunteered at kids' church Sunday morning, lead the welcoming team Sunday night and even sat through mind numbing church board meetings.

Not surprisingly, I suffered a nervous breakdown. I became so physically, emotionally and spiritually exhausted that when I came home from work, all I was capable of doing was flopping on the couch. I had no energy or ability to do anything else. 'Earning' salvation is not a healthy, or necessary, way to live. I finally grasped the words of Matthew 11:28-30 and to this day, I'm overwhelmed with peace every time I read them...

'Are you tired? Worn out? Burned out on religion? Come to me. Get away with me and you'll recover your life. I'll show you how to take a real rest. Walk with me and work with me—watch how I do it. Learn the unforced rhythms of grace. I won't lay anything heavy or ill-fitting on you. Keep company with me and you'll learn to live freely and lightly.'

Once I learnt the 'unforced rhythms of grace,' I was finally able to live 'freely and lightly.' No longer living in fear of losing my salvation, I was able to rest in it and actually enjoy it. I was also much more fun to be around when I switched from 'militant salvation' to a grace-filled relationship with God.

One of the ways the devil tries to trap you is through telling you lies (e.g. the Garden of Eden). And he's so convincing (through millennia of experience!), his lies can be deadly.

When I was about 9 years old, we moved interstate and I started a new school. That's when I met Sarah*. She was a born leader - sporty, charismatic, popular and pretty… All the things I wanted to be. I idolised her and wanted more than anything to be like her.

I styled my hair like her, enunciated my words like her and basically followed her around, as did most of the girls in our grade.

Through high school, our friendship groups changed but after graduation, we found ourselves 'hanging out' again. We started a weekly tradition of catching up on Tuesdays after work, going out for dinner, or watching a movie together. She was pursuing a career in hospitality and had landed a traineeship at one of the fanciest hotels in town. I was still trying to figure out what I wanted to do with my life and was answering phones for a Real Estate Agent while I considered my next step. Her job sounded so fun and exciting, she was progressing through the ranks and was loved by her workmates.

She also had an 'on again off again' boyfriend while I was painfully single.

Then one Monday afternoon I called Sarah to arrange our weekly catch up. Instead of her usual jovial voice on the other end of the phone, she sounded uncharacteristically flat. "What's up?" I asked. "You just interrupted me in the middle of something," she replied. She went on to tell me that she had broken up with her boyfriend again and he was seeing someone else. She said that she had overdue assignments to get on with so it would be a while before we could catch up again. Her last words to me were: "I'll see you soon and speak to you soon."

That's the last time I ever heard her voice.

A couple of hours later her brother found her. Sarah had taken her own life. She was 19. The grief still overwhelms me to this day.

It was the opening line of her suicide note that shocked me most. It read: 'To my family and friends (not many).'

Not many?

Not MANY?

Sarah was the most popular girl in school, *and* in her workplace. Everyone loved Sarah. *Everyone.* Especially me.

But she had believed a lie that the devil had been whispering in her ear, growing to an unbearable **roar** when she felt rejected by her boyfriend.

The lies can come at any time, so you need to be aware and on guard. The whispers started for me one festive season.

There had been a gradual shifting of seasons as my friendship group moved in a different direction, without me. There was no malice, or intentional exclusion. Life is ever changing and during that time of realignment, it felt like I was spinning around in a game of musical chairs, and everyone around me had found their seat. Except me.

Every year, I looked forward to a particular friend's Christmas Party. At each party, there was a new surprise… a waterslide, or a giant, life sized snow globe, food trucks or live entertainment. It was the event of the year for me.

But this year, as the Christmas season progressed, I noticed that an invitation hadn't been forthcoming and I thought, perhaps, that they were having a break this particular year. Until one Friday night, I was at a mutual friend's house for a gathering and I'd brought a cheese platter to share. "We have plenty of cheese," she said, "why don't you take it to the big Christmas Party tomorrow at ---'s house?"

I stood still. She had already moved on, welcoming the next guest. But I was stuck in the moment.

The Christmas Party of the year was tomorrow, and I hadn't been invited. Rejection, loneliness and isolation descended upon me like a sack of potatoes. How odd to feel these emotions surrounded by friends?

Even worse, as I sat down, *everyone* was discussing what treats they would be taking to the big event the following day, naturally assuming that I would be there. But I wouldn't be there. I wasn't invited. I sat still, silent, alone.

I left the gathering early, holding back tears of humiliation and rejection.

Suddenly I was 10 years old again and experiencing the rejection I felt every year when every girl in my class received an invitation to 'the twins' birthday party. Every girl, except me. For whatever reason, these twin girls in my class didn't like me and for whatever reason, every year they invited every girl in the class to their extravagant birthday parties, except me. And it was the birthday party that all the girls talked about every year, except me.

The devil got straight to work. "Nobody likes you. You have no friends." I ugly cried over the kitchen table as my husband tried to comfort me. He doesn't *do* parties, so he was actually relieved that he wasn't expected to attend the event. That didn't make me feel better.

I was starting to believe the same lies that had killed my friend, Sarah: 'To my family and friends (not many).' The weight of rejection sat heavy on my chest and the spiritual battle was fierce.

The bitter root that had seeded there when I was 10 years old, had grown into a nasty weed, strangling the garden of my heart.

How must Jesus have felt when, in his most vulnerable moment, his friends disappeared? How must he have felt in those minutes before the cock crowed three times, watching on from the shame of his cross as one of his very best friends denied ever knowing him?

How did he feel? *"Father, forgive them."* (Luke 23:34)

Of course, God is far too kind to leave me reeling in a state of misery. Not long after the events of that ill-fated festive season, a lovely friend sent me this message: *"I wanted to let you know that I woke in the middle of the night last night with you on my mind/heart. I prayed for you and while I was praying, I felt there's been a pattern of Rejection in your life lately. So I prayed against that in the name of Jesus. God sees and knows exactly how that has made you feel and He is with you, feeling your pain."*

What joy to see and feel seen by God.

It can be tempting to try and change your identity in order to feel accepted. I was chatting with a colleague one day and he said, "You know, I believe we have three identities; There's who we are when we're with friends, who we are when we're with strangers and who we are when we're alone." I paused for a moment, pondering this idea. Then I replied, "You have one identity and I know exactly who you are." His eyes widened. "Would you like me to tell you who you are?" He hesitated, then nodded. "You are loved. That's who you are. That's your identity. And when you fully grasp that, you will be exactly the same person, regardless of whether you're surrounded by friends, strangers, or you're by yourself." Tears welled in his eyes. "No one's ever said that to me before," he said. "I can feel a huge weight dropping from my shoulders just knowing that. He went on to explain that he'd just spent months in a mental health facility, following a nervous breakdown. The burden of pretending and transitioning like a chameleon to fit into his surroundings had become too great to carry.

When I became a wife, I changed my last name to reflect my new 'identity.' And one of the many surprises about becoming a mother was discovering that my name had changed once again. No longer was I called AJ, but instead I became known, in many circles, simply and seamlessly as 'Tyson's mum.' I gladly accepted my new title. Becoming a mother has been the greatest joy and honour of my life. In some cultures, a mother's name changes officially at the birth of her first son. So, I would forever be known as 'Mother of Tyson.'

Now at school drop off, I hear happy little voices call out "Hi Tyson's mum." Or "Hey Jack's mum, can Jack come over for a play date?" And I'm guilty of entering other mums' names in my phone as 'Marree – Nate's mum,' or 'Suellen – Tyler's mum.' It's as though when we gave birth to our children, we birthed a new 'identity' ourselves.

Perhaps your own 'identity' doesn't sit so well with you. Perhaps someone close to you has told you that your identity is 'unwanted,' 'hopeless,' or 'loser.' Or perhaps, like the prisoners and people struggling with addiction I've interviewed, your actions have defined your identity. Adulterer, murderer, thief.

You're in good company. These words once defined King David. He stole another man's wife, slept with her, then murdered her husband (2 Samuel 7-12). But when David repented, his sins no longer defined him, or his children.

You will no doubt have heard of King Solomon, David's son. But did you know he had two names?

'God had a special love for him and sent word by Nathan the prophet that God wanted him named Jedidiah (God's Beloved).' 2 Samuel 12:25

My favourite of the four gospels is the Book of John. He writes about Jesus as someone who really knew him and thoroughly adored him. Six times throughout his gospel, John refers to himself as 'the disciple whom Jesus loved.' Does that mean Jesus didn't love the others? Not at all. It's just that John embraced his true, unchanging identity.

How fun it would be to introduce myself to strangers, "Hey, I'm AJ, God's Beloved." And how true it is!

Regardless of marital status, career status, friendship status, your past, how many kids you have, or whether you have kids at all, your true identity in Christ remains unchanged into eternity; you are 'God's Beloved.'

*I've changed the name of my precious friend to protect the privacy of her family.

Bibliography

1. Awe expands people's perception of time, alters decision making, and enhances well-being. Rudd M, Aaker J and Vohs K. in press. *Psychological Science.*
2. Relationships Among Positive Emotions, Coping, Resilience and Mental Health. Christian T. Gloria & Mary A. Steinhardt
3. Unskilled and unaware of it: how difficulties in recognizing one's own incompetence lead to inflated self-assessments. J. Kruger, D. Dunning. Published 1999. Journal of personality and social psychology
4. From Jerusalem to Jericho: A study of Situational and Dispositional Variables in Helping Behavior. Darley, J. M., and Batson, C.D. (1973). Journal of Personality and Social Psychology, 1973, 27, 100-108.
5. When I Survey the Wondrous Cross: Words by Isaac Watts, music by Lowell Mason
6. Parrots Voluntarily Help Each Other to Obtain Food Rewards – Current Biology VOLUME 30, ISSUE 2, P292-297. E5, JANUARY 20, 2020
7. It Is Well with My Soul: Words by Horatio G. Spafford, music by Philip P. Bliss
8. Tolkien, J. R. R. The Two Towers. HarperCollins, 2005.

9   Is more always better?: A survey on positional concerns. Solnick and Hemenway (1997). Journal of Economic Behavior and Organization, 37, 373-383.

www.ingramcontent.com/pod-product-compliance
Lightning Source LLC
LaVergne TN
LVHW051133080426
835510LV00018B/2392